GW00660296

WORDS THAT SELL CARS

PROVEN WORD TRACKS TO
TRANSFORM YOUR SALES TEAM'S
PERFORMANCE & **IMPROVE**
YOUR BOTTOM LINE, FAST!

SIMON BOWKETT

First published in Great Britain 2019
by Rethink Press (www.rethinkpress.com)

© Copyright Simon Bowkett

All rights reserved. No part of this publication may be reproduced, stored in or introduced into a retrieval system, or transmitted, in any form, or by any means (electronic, mechanical, photocopying, recording or otherwise) without the prior written permission of the publisher.

The right of Simon Bowkett to be identified as the author of this work has been asserted by him in accordance with the Copyright, Designs and Patents Act 1988.

This book is sold subject to the condition that it shall not, by way of trade or otherwise, be lent, resold, hired out, or otherwise circulated without the publisher's prior consent in any form of binding or cover other than that in which it is published and without a similar condition including this condition being imposed on the subsequent purchaser.

Cover image © Shutterstock – TheModernCanvas

Contents

Introduction

There's a cliché in the world of sales training: those who can, do; those who can't, teach. But is there any truth in that saying? I think there is, and if I'm brutally honest, I'm writing this book precisely because of that statement.

I started in the motor trade when I was seventeen years old. I was one of those cadet salespeople, spending twelve months making the teas and the coffees, and taking people for demonstration drives. I also spent a little bit of time in the service department speaking to customers. In 1995, I left Australia to come to the UK, where I found myself in a Nissan dealership in High Wycombe as the sales manager. When a guy from the manufacturer turned up to do some training with my salespeople, I said to him, 'I like the idea of on-site training and coaching, but before you start can you talk me through your sales process?'

I thought it was a fair question – I wanted to make sure we were on the same page. The guy replied: 'Yeah, sure I can do that for you, no problem. First it's meet and greet, then it's qualification of the customer's needs and wants, and oh, I'm sorry I always forget this one…' and he did a nervous dive into his briefcase trying to find his sales process.

As you can imagine, alarm bells went off in my head. I asked him when he had last actually sold a car in the real world, and his response was: 'Well, I've had placement.' I was left scratching my head wondering what the hell a 'placement' was. So I asked him. It turned out placement meant when he left university, he went into a car dealership for two months to learn how the process worked. I was a cocky, young sales manager back then and replied sarcastically, 'Oh great, was that two whole months? And now you're going to teach my guys how to sell a car?'

You learn very quickly in the motor industry that sometimes you have to tell the manufacturer what they want to hear to get the right dealer operating standards. And that's what I did with this guy. I added, 'Right, and in that two months I'm sure you sold lots of cars.'

But I lost the will to live when he said, 'Oh no, no! I wasn't at that level. I was at management level. I was doing what you're doing. I was looking at man management, and motivation, and KPIs – the key performance indicators.'

He'd never actually sold a car.

By this time, I was really nervous, so I asked him to take me through the training he was planning on teaching my guys – and while I couldn't knock the content that he was planning to teach my salespeople, I was worried about him as the person doing the training.

On day one he was doing telephone training in a little glass office off the side of my office. He was in there with one of my salespeople when a telephone inquiry came through. This was my opportunity: I ducked my head around the corner and said: 'Hey, Mr Trainer, can you do me a favour? Instead of telling my salesperson how to do it, why don't you show him.'

Guess what colour he went? You could almost see the shite running down the backs of his legs. He then threw in a lovely, consultant face-saver, saying 'What I prefer to do is let your salesperson take the call, and then I can critique him.'

Anyone can tell someone how they've got it wrong *after* the fact. Show him how to do it correctly right from the start. Guys, I can tell you where the Australian Rugby team went wrong with their last game, but if you looked at me, you'd know I couldn't play myself! But, bless him, this turkey refused to take the call and responded, 'Well, I'm only here once a month, so why don't I coach you on how to take the call and critique you?'

My response? Well, full disclosure, I don't recommend you do this to anyone from your manufacturer or your dealer group, because I got in a lot of trouble. I was just a salesperson and I was worried about the incoming telephone inquiry, so I asked my sales guy to take the call. I pulled the trainer back to my office and said: 'Right, Mr Trainer, do me a favour, get on your bike and leave.' Though to be honest with you, those might not be the *exact* words I used! I've matured (slightly) since those days – but, even now, I'd do exactly the same thing.

If you're getting sales training, make sure you ask the trainer when was the last time they sold anything in the real world. Why? The market's changing all the time. When I started selling cars my job as a salesperson was almost like being a teacher. Customers would ask lots of questions: 'Tell me about this car, tell me what this one's got.' But now customers tell me they know exactly what they want: 'I want that Audi, S-Line plus, with the big alloy wheels, and I want the active lane departure warning system.' They know more about the car than we do sometimes. You need to be taking sales training advice from people who are doing it right now!

In this book I'm going to talk about ideas being put into practice in the real world. In our business we do a whole lot of R and D. You might think that means research and development – but we call it Rob and Duplicate. If there's a good idea out there, I'll rob it and duplicate it – and come and tell you about it. Of course, I'll always tell you where I've nicked the ideas from and give credit to the right people.

I'm going to introduce you to plenty of ideas that you can immediately implement, including the four fundamentals that must be met for success in sales. I'll show you some of my favourite and most successful word tracks. But, do me a favour, *never* use any of the words or word tracks exactly how you see them – you'll just sound like a cheesy Aussie! I want you to take these ideas, take the meaning, then change and shape it to make it right for *your* customers and *your* industry.

That's why I'm going to talk about the psychology behind some of these word tracks. For each waypoint on the Road to a Sale there will be word tracks for you to use. You can respond one of three ways to them: If you like them send me an email telling me so (that's great for my ego); or, if you don't like them, tell me that too – because who says I'm right? I'm just going to tell you what's worked well for me and other salespeople.

The third response you might have is 'bollocks!' If you've been jaded by too many courses, with the grey-haired old guy up front telling his war stories about what he did in 1992, you might nod politely but you're probably thinking, 'I'd like to see him do that in the real world.' If you're in the third camp, don't worry, just pick what's right for you. This book is packed with useful insights, and I'm sure you'll find something you can use.

From Camels to Clicks

Let's have a look at how the world has changed. When people were trading camels in the desert 2,000 years ago, would it be much different to what we do today? They would, at least, have to have the right attitude. If we went in to buy a camel and the camel trader said, 'Sorry, it's almost closing time, come back next week,' we probably wouldn't go back next week. Attitude comes first.

Secondly, we'd have to say hello with some sort of meet and greet. I bet that even 2,000 years ago we'd still have customers say, 'No, no. I'm just looking – just kicking a few hooves around.' We'd have to open them up. But I also reckon 2,000 years ago someone would ask, 'Right, what's the best price on that camel right now? Cash, no trade-in. What can you do?' We'd have to slow them down.

Wouldn't we have to qualify the customer's needs and wants 2,000 years ago? Of course we would. 'What are you looking for? A one-humper or two-humper? Are you looking for camels for short hauls across a market or long hauls across the desert?' We'd ask them questions, like 'How are you getting your goods around at the moment? Donkey? Great!' We'd probably use the customer's current situation as a qualifier too:

> **'So, what do you like most about donkeys?'**
> 'They're cheap.'
>
> *Hmm, a price conscious man. Probably wants a Dacia camel.*
>
> **'What don't you like about donkeys?'**
> 'They keep dying in the desert.'
>
> **Well, that's a problem we can offer a solution to.**
>
> **'Why are you looking to change?'**
> 'I've been carrying around frankincense and myrrh and I'm transferring to gold for the next Christmas season, so I need a little bit more carrying capacity.'
> **'Ah, you sound like a very wise man, Sir. Come with me, I've got a good deal on this beige one at the moment.'**

We could then go into the presentation of the camel. 'Have a look at this one, it's a Sahara Desert version. It's got double the amount of water because it's got two humps. You're not going to have to stop at the oasis and miss an important event. Have a look at the size of the hooves, it will never sink into quicksand!'

I don't know, I've never sold a camel, but I reckon 2,000 years ago that the salesperson would have to present the camel. Would they do a demonstration or a test ride 2,000 years ago? Probably! There would likely be some sort of trial close or commitment, because if the camel didn't do the job the person is looking for, would it matter how cheap it was? 'Listen, if we get the exchange right is this camel going to suit what you're looking for?'

These stages of the process wouldn't be any different. I believe that from the start of time, whoever is buying the camel will always want to pay as little as they possibly can. Whoever is selling the camel would want to get as much as they can.

> **'I'll give you three pigs and my mother-in-law for that camel.'**
>
> 'No, your mother-in-law is a pig. I want seven pigs and your best-looking, youngest wife.'

Two thousand years ago we'd have customers saying, 'OK, well that's food for thought. I never buy a camel on the first day. I just want to sleep on it.'

Two thousand years ago you'd probably get a customer saying, 'Well hold on, I'll stop you right there. I've been down the road to Camel-Wow and they're doing them a lot cheaper. You'll have to sharpen up your pencil.'

Two thousand years ago, people might say, 'What? Two pigs for my donkey? Are you on drugs? Everyone knows that a donkey is worth more than two pigs. Do you know what I paid for that donkey?'

The sales process has been around for a long time. However, there's one thing that we have to put up with now that the camel sales person never had to 2,000 years ago. What do you think it is? The internet. Everyone does research before they make a purchase. Some customers now go straight from the meet and greet stage into, 'Listen, I know what I want. All I want to know is your best price right now – cash, no trade-in.'

Years ago, I was told to raise the desire with a demonstration drive, and I still believe in that. We used to say to people, 'Come on Sir, you wouldn't buy a pair of shoes without trying them on first. And a car is more important than a pair of shoes.' Guess what. People still buy shoes – but now it's online!

No one would ever buy a car from a vending machine, would they? Go online and look at Carvana.com. This company has somewhere between 10,000 to 12,000 used cars in stock. The customer goes online and gets a virtual demonstration, a presentation of each and every car. They highlight any damage on the car. They go straight to presenting the deal and show the customer how much a month they'll need to pay, what deposit they need, and the actual interest rate on the loan. When the customer agrees to buy, Carvana sends the car overnight to wherever in America that customer is living. The next day, in the post, a big silver coin turns up. The customer goes to the car vending machine, puts the coin in the slot, and the car they bought the day before trundles out, like a Mars bar!

Does this mean we don't need salespeople anymore? The world is changing, this car vending machine exists right now – but people still need to speak to people, for the trust and the rapport.

There are aircraft nowadays that can take off, navigate the whole journey and land – without the pilot touching anything. I read recently that all they need in a modern aeroplane is a pilot and a dog. The dog to bite the pilot if he touches anything, and the pilot to feed the dog. They have these automatic planes out there, but are you ready to get on a plane without a pilot sitting in the front? No, me neither. Now, for our children it might be different, they might get used to it, but I still believe that people need to speak to people for trust and rapport.

I heard one of the Directors at Carvana say that even though people can click and go through the whole process without speaking to a human, it's rarer then you may think. Even now, with new technology and the internet, people still want and need to speak to people. In this book we'll look at the process for the modern world and we'll talk about the word tracks that you can use to deal with the whole sales process.

PART ONE

IT'S ALL IN THE MIND

ONE

The Four Fundamentals

L et's start with the basics. There are four fundamentals of sales that have to be satisfied for your customer to buy – at least where 'big-ticket' items are concerned. If any one of them are not satisfied within the customer's mind, they're not going to buy. These fundamentals help influence the customer's decision to part with their cash. You may succeed in the sale by just using one, but let's aim to satisfy as many as we can. These four fundamentals are: comparison, value, scarcity, and urgency. The right combination at the right time can help you make the sale – and ensure the customer is satisfied.

Comparison

If you ask someone who has just bought a house, 'Did you get a good deal?' invariably they will say yes, otherwise they wouldn't have bought it. But how do they know? When I ask people these questions, I usually hear one of two responses:

1. 'Yes, I got a good deal and I know because the house down the road was for sale at £150,000, the one next door was for sale for £160,000, and I bought mine for £140,000. It was a great deal.' This is called shopping around. Do you really want your customers to shop around? Probably not!

2. 'Yeah, I got a cracking deal because… it was up for £350,000 and I got it for £300,000.' This is about the discount they got. But how does the customer know £350,000 was the right price to start with?

In the first example, the person shopped around and felt they got a good deal. In the second, they felt like they got a discount – and so must have got a good deal. But how do they know the £350,000 was the right price to start with?

The first fundamental is comparison. For someone to feel like they've got a good deal, they need to compare it to something else. We don't want our customers shopping around, nor looking for discounts. If they shop around, they might find someone willing to give away some of their margin and sell for a lot less than we want to. And, from a customer's point of view, they might not be comparing apples with apples.

Retailers are great at the fundamental of using comparison to their advantage. There are always 'sales' on at furniture retailers, where the sofa that usually costs £2,000 is just £1,000. Or that plasma screen TV at the electrical store, which is normally £1,500, for this weekend is only £750 – so buy it now while stocks last. My wife is brilliant at comparison shopping, 'Look at these shoes I bought, I saved £100.' She didn't save £100, she spent £300. She decided she got a good deal because of the amount of discount she was told she got. And while we all know that Furniture Village is going to have another sale next week, we worry that they might sell out, or the discount won't be as big. We fear the loss. It's a fundamental of human nature to decide we got a good deal by how much we 'saved'.

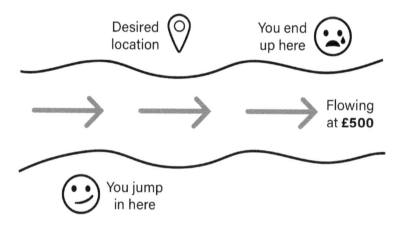

Desired location

You end up here

Flowing at **£500**

You jump in here

Figure 1.1 The negotiating river

Sometimes this is referred to as anchoring; a cognitive bias that occurs in decision making when we rely too heavily on the first piece of information we receive, or the anchor. A great example of the power of comparison is a study by Cialdini, et al, in 1975.[1] The researchers asked students to volunteer one two-hour session per week for two years of their life as a counsellor. Most of the students said no thanks (that's a lot of beer-drinking time at university). They then were asked to volunteer just one two-hour session. Nearly half of the students said OK. The comparison between two hours per week for two years of their life to just one two-hour session

---

1   Cialdini, R.B., Vincent, J.E., Lewis, S.K., Catalan, J., Wheeler, D., & Darby, B.L., *Reciprocal Concessions Procedure for Inducing Compliance: The door-in-the-face technique.* JPSP, 1975,31,206-215.

seemed like a good deal. They then asked a control group to volunteer just the one two-hour session, without first being conditioned (or anchored) by the larger request. Only seventeen percent of them agreed! How can we make this work for us? Let's have a look at the negotiating river.

You're standing on the south bank of the negotiating river and you want to get to the north bank, directly opposite where you are standing now – but the river is flowing from left to right. If you jumped in and started swimming, the current would take you downstream. To come out at your desired point, you have to jump in the river upstream knowing that the current is going to take you downstream. Your upstream jumping-in point is the anchor.

The researchers chucked the first group of students in the river at two hours per week for two years of their life – the anchor. The students came out of the river at just one two-hour session – the comparison made them feel good. The control group were chucked in the river at one two-hour session and had nothing to compare against. They didn't feel it was a good deal, so only seventeen percent took them up on it.

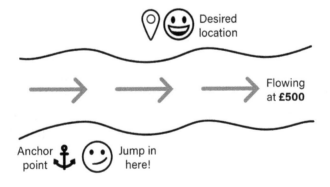

Figure 1.2 Negotiating river anchor

What about the movement of money? Assume our negotiating river is flowing by £500, which means the customer needs to see £500 worth of movement before they feel like they got a good deal. Look at this next image:

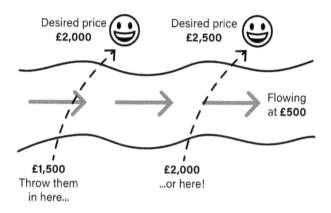

Figure 1.3 Negotiating river movement

Let's say we want to give the customer £2,000 for the car they're trading-in. If we just gave them £2,000 for their car, they won't feel satisfied – they'd want at least £2,500 before they felt like they'd got a good deal and the fundamental need for comparison was satisfied. If you want the customer to come out of the river at £2,000, you need to throw them in the river at £1,500.

Now, here's something to think about: even if you gave the customer £2,500 to start with, they wouldn't be happy. They'd want £3,000 before they felt like they got a good deal and could satisfy the fundamental need for comparison (of course, that's unless they haven't already shopped around). It's the movement that's important – you need to provide them with an anchor. If you can't satisfy your customer's fundamental need for comparison, they're going to have to satisfy it by going elsewhere and shopping around.

The law of comparison is so strong that sometimes we do it *after* we have bought something. This happened to me recently when I kicked my laptop off the desk and broke it in two. Not in a rage or anything. I was walking past my laptop at a thousand miles per hour, caught the cable, and my laptop spun around and smashed. I had a gig in Germany on Monday morning, so I needed a new one quickly. I went to my local store and bought the first model that satisfied my computing needs. I didn't have time to shop around as I had so little time. As I'm walking through the airport with my new computer, I see a retailer there selling the same model. Do you think I had a look at how much they were selling it for? Of course I did. The urge was too strong – and I knew I was just going to be upset when I saw the price was £100 cheaper.

That's how powerful the law of comparison is.

Remember, a thing is only worth what someone's willing to pay for it. And what someone has already paid sets the market. The housing and financial crisis in the 2000s was in part caused by the fundamental of comparison. Here's just one example. Developers built blocks of flats in the middle of Manchester worth £200,000. The developer wanted to make as much money as he could, so he guaranteed buyers the rental income on the flats for the next two years and offered to pay their deposit. But, of course, the sales price was set at £240,000, and the developer didn't tell the buyer that the flat was really only worth £200,000.

But how did the developer convince the buyer, and more importantly the lending bank, that a £200,000 unit was really worth £240,000? They used the fundamental of comparison.

They sold one of these apartments in the block of flats to themselves for £250,000. They sold another one to themselves for £255,000. When the buyer and the bank did their due diligence and looked at recent sales prices, £240,000 looked like a great deal. They artificially created a situation that could be used for the law of comparison.

This was a scam and I don't condone this.

But this scam worked well for years – until there was a glut of flats built. As each flat owner's rental income guarantee expired, they had to lower their rental prices to get renters. The owners fell afoul of the fundamental of comparison as renters shopped around looking for a better deal. The owners continued to lower their rent to the point that the income didn't pay the mortgage – they needed to sell. So they asked the local estate agents what their flats were worth: the flats were worth what someone was willing to pay. Buyers found out that flats had been selling for less than £200,000 as the developers sold up their flats in the block and hot-footed it to Barbados. Their £240,000 investment was only worth £200,000. In part this is how toxic debt built up around the Western world.

Remember, we must satisfy the customer's fundamental need for comparison. If not, they'll go and buy from someone else.

Value

Would you pay £50,000 for a watch? What about £25,000? You might be thinking I'm on drugs – you can tell the time from your iPhone, why would you need a £25,000 watch? OK, seriously, would you pay £50 for a watch? During one of my training courses, I got right down to £1 before anyone offered to buy the watch. I had to discount £49,999 before I could secure the deal. That's really bad negotiation on my part, but great negotiation on the buyer's part. This happens all too frequently to the poor salesperson – because they're not using the fundamental of value to sell that product or service, they're using the fundamental of comparison. You're devaluing your product by using comparison alone.

If a thing is only worth what someone is willing to pay for it, how do you show a customer the value in your product or service?

Think about a set of value scales. On one side we have the product or service, whether that's a house, a car, a watch or a diamond, and on the other side we've got the amount of money we have to spend to get it. If the amount of money a customer needs to spend is too high, it outweighs the value of the product or service, and they're never going to buy it. What we need is the value of the product or service to outweigh the amount of money that's spent on it.

Figure 1.4 Value scales

Value is always a perception. What's anything worth? It's worth what someone's willing to pay for it. We walk into an electrical shop and hand over lots of pieces of paper and they hand us a plasma screen TV. Are those pieces of paper really worth £20? It's all about the perception of what something is worth. If we build more perceived value in the product or service, the amount of money that the customer needs to spend will seem like less.

Let's get back to that watch. I didn't tell you anything about the watch, did I? I didn't attempt to build any value on the watch. Now, the watch I was actually trying to sell you is by Patek Philippe, and this particular model is one of only two that were ever made. It is one of two platinum 2499s created for Mr Philippe Stern, the Managing Director of the company. The one I'm trying to sell you was owned by Eric Clapton and sold at a Christie's auction in 2013 for 3.6 million US dollars.

Now, for *that* watch, would you give me £50,000? You'd probably do all you could to find £50,000. You'd probably rush off down to the bank and re-mortgage your over-priced flat in Manchester. You'd speak to parents and friends because you know that £50,000 watch is worth a lot more.

But is that watch worth 3.6 million US dollars? It might not seem worth that to you or me, but someone is willing to pay that for it, and so that is its worth.

What would you pay for a dusty old violin from a second-hand music shop? £25, £50, maybe £100? Until you dust it off, clean it up and see, stamped on the side, that it's a Stradivarius. What's it worth now? It's actually worth a small fortune. You may have heard about the classic violinist, Min-Jin Kym, who owned a Stradivarius violin, valued at $1.2 million. She accidentally left it in a sandwich shop, a Pret a Manger in the middle of London. A man called John Maughan took the violin.

In 2011, Maughan went to jail over the theft of that violin. The most interesting thing is how they actually caught him. They caught him because he advertised it on Ebay. He had a buy-it-now price. What do you think it was? £1 million... half a million? Maybe £100,000? No, he had a buy-it-now price of £100. He had no idea what it was worth. Before he was caught, he was getting on a bus with this violin. The bus driver said, 'Oh, my daughter started playing music at school. I need to get her something.' He said to the bus driver, 'Well, you can have this if you want, for 50 quid.' And the bus driver said, 'No. She's got a recorder, that'll do her.' That $1.2 million violin could have changed hands for £50.

Is that violin really worth $1.2 million? Not to me, maybe not to you, but it *is* worth that: because value is what someone's willing to pay for it.

Professor Robert Cialdini noted in his bestselling book, *Influence*, that the principles of material self-interest were not included in his research, because people wanting to maximize the benefit and reduce the costs is a given. We all want more for less. Harvey Golub and Jane Henry of McKinsey & Company said in their 1981 staff paper 'Market strategy and the price-value model', that a product's value to a customer is simply the greatest amount of money they would be willing to pay for it. However, they also said the value depends on the customer's subjective assessment of that product. How the customer *feels*.

Legend has it that Picasso was in a Paris café when a woman approached him and asked, 'Would you draw me something please?' He drew an image of a dove on a napkin. It took him about 30 seconds. He handed the drawing to her and requested a significant amount of francs. The lady was shocked, 'What? It took you 30 seconds to draw it.' And the master said something along the lines of, 'No. That didn't take me 30 seconds to draw, that took me 40 years of my life.' Picasso was claiming the value not only in the drawing 'The Dove of Peace', he was claiming value in his expertise and his time.

We need to build value on our product or our service. And value is always a perception.

There's a series of fifteen paintings titled *Les Femmes d'Alger* or *Women of Algiers* by Picasso and, while I'm not an art critic, I'm not sure I'd really want any of them hanging on a wall at home. But I guess most people would love *Les Femmes d'Alger* (version O) hanging on the wall because they could take it down, sell it and clear the mortgage on their flat in Manchester! It sold at Christie's Auction in New York for $179 million.

Why is it worth $179 million? What usually has to happen for an artist to become wealthy? They have to die! Scarcity (the third fundamental) adds value. Which leads me to one of my heroes, Damien Hirst. This is the guy that's famous for painting coloured round dots and for cutting animals in half and displaying them in two Perspex boxes. He's also the guy that floated a shark in a big tank of formaldehyde. Don't get me wrong, I don't really like the idea of dead animals cut in two – but to each their own. It's not my thing at all but he's still my hero. Just after they sold the shark for $3 million, interviewer Evan Davis asked, 'Is that really worth $3 million?' Hirst replied, 'What's anything worth? I give up guessing what something's worth. It's only worth what someone's willing to pay for it. If two people have a lot of money and they want to buy it, it's going to sell for a lot of money.'

One of my clients pointed out that the real hero behind Damien Hirst was his manager, who taught him to use scarcity to build value. In fact, Damien Hirst's step-father was a car salesperson. Damien Hirst can build value in shite.

Thinking about our artists, to earn a lot of money as an artist you normally have to die. It's only when the artist dies that their work becomes scarce, which we'll cover in more depth in the next fundamental.

Scarcity

Scarcity is what makes a diamond valuable. A diamond is just a pretty rock, but are they really worth what we pay for them? What makes them valuable is their scarcity. If there were enough diamonds so that every man, woman, and child could have as many as they wanted, their value would plummet.

This is also referred to as supply and demand. If something is scarce, someone might pay more for it. If there's restricted supply, there might be more demand. If there's more demand, people might pay more for it. It's a vicious circle. If we had an infinite diamond mine, we might benefit from holding back the supply of diamonds, only releasing a small amount to the market at a time, in order to create scarcity. By artificially managing supply (creating scarcity) we create demand.

Luxury goods manufacturers understand this principle. Rolex produce the Rolex Daytona watch, which they claim has a seven-year wait list. Do you think that maybe Rolex is drip feeding the market, creating scarcity so that people really want – and so will pay more for – them?

Let's take a look at the science behind scarcity, or artificially manipulating supply and demand. Back in 1975, a study was done on the effects of supply and demand and ratings of objective values, and it was published in the Journal of Personality and Social Psychology.[2] The researchers, Worchel, Lee and Adewole, set up an experiment where they asked 200 undergraduates to rate chocolate chip cookies on attractiveness and taste. The cookies were displayed in two jars – one jar was almost empty (scarce) and the second jar was almost full (abundant). The students were asked to enter the room and identify which cookies appeared better. The cookies in scarce supply were repeatedly rated better than those in abundant supply. If everyone else is going for it, it must be the best! People want what everyone else wants, and this affected people's perception of the cookie before they even tasted it. The cookies were, in fact, identical. The lure of scarcity means we want it before it's gone.

Imagine you're on holiday in Spain walking along the seafront: are you going to choose the restaurant that's empty? You might think that as no one else is there you'd get served straight away and probably get great service from the waiting staff. But no, we tend to go to the restaurant that's busy, because if everyone else is eating there it must be good. Scarcity was a factor in the Manchester flats con. Who knew if more would be built, there's only so much real estate.

You know what? We often want what we can't have. If everyone else wants it, we want it. I got a great lesson in scarcity with my wife, Emma, ten years ago. We were looking to buy a house and found one that stacked up on what we're looking for: near the right schools, great space inside… but it was ugly. However you looked at it, it was ugly. If we bought, it we'd have to do a

---

2   Worchel, S., Lee, J. & Adewole, A. (1975). Effects of supply and demand on ratings of object value. *Journal of Personality and Social Psychology*, 32(5), 906-914.

lot of work on the outside. I said to Emma, 'Let's offer £50,000 less because we'd need to spend at least that much to make the front look better, or maybe hide it with a lot of trees.'

My conversation with the estate agent went something like this:

> 'Hi. Yes, I'd like to make an offer on that house.'
>
> 'Oh, sorry. It's sold.'
>
> 'What if I offered the full asking price?'
>
> 'No.'
>
> 'Okay. I'd have to go over full asking price?'

Emma, only hearing half the conversation, was shaking her head and laughing at me!

In a heartbeat, I went from wanting to offer £50,000 less to being prepared to offer more. What changed was the scarcity – it was available before and now it wasn't. Which brings us to the last fundamental – urgency.

Urgency

What if you're selling a product that's not scarce? The motor industry pumps out cars as fast as Subway throws out foot-longs. So, what do you do if your industry isn't naturally scarce? If you're selling Ferraris you have scarcity and exclusivity, but for most car sales you have to do something different.

Let's have a look at water. In a restaurant we might insist on only having tap water (who wants to pay for bottled water in a restaurant?) but then we go shopping for bottled water to drink at home. Why do we pay for bottled water at home?

One, we know it's going to be clean. It's also convenient and comes in a nice bottle. But at the end of the day, it's water, and water for most people in the civilized world isn't scarce! So how much would you pay for 500 ml of clean, convenient water? If you buy it in bulk at a wholesaler, it might work out to 50p. If you buy it at a Subway restaurant it might be £1.50 for the same bottle of water. If you buy it at a club in Ibiza, you could end up paying £10.00 – for exactly the same bottle! Has the product changed? No – the situation has changed. Do you think I'd ever be able to persuade you to pay £100 for that 500 ml bottle of water? Of course I could, in a heartbeat. All I need to do is bring in the fourth fundamental, urgency.

Let's say you're in the middle of the desert, you haven't had a drink for days, and you've got to survive six more hours before you'll be rescued. Some old guy comes along on a camel with a one litre bottle full of water. How much would you give him for it? You'd give him the hundred pounds, wouldn't you? You'd give him everything you had. You'd probably give him that Picasso painting, your violin, your new laptop and your flat in Manchester. You'd definitely give him that shark in the formaldehyde tank. You'd give him everything. What changed? Urgency.

We need to create urgency throughout the deal, but there's a problem. Customers don't always believe the urgency. There's a saying, *what's for you won't go by you*, so plenty of people won't buy in to faked urgency. Urgency needs to be subtle, believable, and introduced early on in the process. Customers don't believe you when you throw in some urgency at the end.

I remember a couple of years ago, between Christmas and New Year's, my wife wanted to buy a new blouse. I'm not a 'shopper' at the best of times, but my heart sank – the Boxing

Day sales were on, and it was one of the busiest shopping days of the year.

Now, where I live I had some choices. Number one – take her to the Trafford Centre, one of the biggest shopping centres in the world which would be rammed. Forget that! Number two, take her to my hell on earth, Cheshire Oaks, an outdoor outlet village in the cold, the wet, and the rain. That would probably be worse than the shopping mall. Or, the third choice, we could slope off to Tarporley, a mile and a half down the road, with some small boutique shops where I knew I'd spend more money, but we'd get in, get what she wants, and get out. The kids were away at the in-laws, so we could go and have a lovely pub lunch, a bubbly glass of Prosecco for her, and I'd get a nice cold pint in a frosted glass. Perfect weekend.

We went to The Wardrobe in Tarporley, perfectly named because it's tiny, not much bigger than a triple car garage. It's run by a lovely, helpful lady and thankfully there's a 'man chair' – that chair in the corner for the husbands to sit down in. I plonked myself down and flicked through some sports stuff on my phone while Emma flicked through the blouses.

She found one she liked.

'What do you think?'

I made the mistake of saying, 'That's fine.' Clearly what I meant by *fine* was, 'Wow, that was quick. The first shop and she's found something she likes, now let's get out of here.'

Of course, what Emma thought when I said fine was, 'Fine? He's not sure. If he's not sure, maybe I'm not sure. I'll keep looking.' And she hung it back up on the rack. In my head I was screaming, 'Noooo!' and I was panicking at my schoolboy error. I knew I'd end up being dragged to the Trafford Centre, then Cheshire Oaks, and at about 4:00 pm I'd probably hear, 'You know what, I think I preferred the first one, let's go back and get that.' And that pub lunch would be lost forever.

Just when I thought all was lost, I was saved – by urgency. Another woman walked into the shop and picked up the same blouse that was in Emma's hand two minutes earlier. Emma's head spun around like a scene out of *The Exorcist*, and I know in her mind she was thinking, 'Bitch, I was looking at that, and if my stupid husband had said it was perfect, I'd have it by now and I'd be drinking a lovely Prosecco.' Thankfully she didn't say this out loud! But I knew what she was thinking.

My Saturday was saved when this other woman wasn't sure either and put it back on the rack. What did Emma do? She marched straight over there and bought the blouse. The funny thing is, I've never seen Emma wear that blouse. People want what they can't have. That's that fundamental of urgency. In sales it's often called the take away close.

Psychologists know that urgent situations cause humans to suspend deliberate thought and to act quickly. Daniel Kahneman, widely regarded as the most influential living psychologist, said that 'losses loom larger than gains'.[3] Would you work harder to earn an extra five dollars, or to stop me from stealing five dollars from you? Which would be the bigger motivator? For most people it's the fear of loss. Urgency can be seen as the fear of, or reducing the pain of, a loss. People don't want to miss out on that product or that service. What's the difference between the fundamental of scarcity and the fundamental of urgency? Scarcity is something like

---

3   Kahneman, D., & Tversky, A. (1979). Prospect theory: An analysis of decision under risk. *Econometrica, 47*, 263-291.

a diamond or a painting by Picasso – there's not that many of them. Urgency has a time element – and is often something we need to create.

Let's use selling cars as an example. The fundamental of scarcity is invoked when there's one used car that the buyer wants, and there's not many of that make or model available. Urgency occurs when the MOT test is coming up and they're worried about it not passing. Or perhaps their in-laws are coming out from Australia and they want a new car before they turn up.

Urgency needs to be subtle, believable, and introduced early on – and it will affect your ability to sell the product.

Now, let's have a look at the four fundamentals together.

The Four Fundamentals Working Together

I was on holiday recently with my family in Florida and we went to Universal's Volcano Bay. This water park had just opened and my boys were really excited to go. On this particular day, James, my oldest, was sick so he stayed at the hotel with Emma. So it was just Sean and me going to the water park, and we were going to have a ball. We turned up there nice and early because we wanted to get on as many rides as we could. What we didn't realise is the park opened up an hour earlier for the people who were staying in the Bay, and as we walked in it was already overcrowded.

We walked past two Scottish ladies really kicking off because they had nowhere to sit. They were talking to a security guard saying they weren't going anywhere until he found them somewhere to sit. I thought that was strange, but it soon became evident what actually happened.

We got changed and went to the first ride. This water park uses TapuTapus, wristbands that work in conjunction with the virtual lines so you know how long you have to wait to ride. You 'tap' into the ride and it tells you what time you need to come back to it to start queuing for the ride. We went to the first water slide, tapped into it and it informed us we needed to wait three hours to ride! Three hours! Forget that, we'll go to the next ride.

We looked at the other rides and the shortest time to ride we could find was an hour and a half virtual wait. Now, let me tell you what that means. That means you have to wait for an hour and a half before you're allowed to get into the queue to wait for the ride. This place was rammed to capacity – there were 7,500 people in this water park. It was 39 degrees, baking hot and there was nowhere to sit. We tried to find some chairs, but the only place we could sit was on the rubber rings floating around in the rapids. Even that was overcrowded. Or we could go into one of the restaurants and have their over-priced meals. I was knackered, I needed to sit somewhere – I couldn't disappoint Sean, he was so excited.

Then I noticed they had these little cabanas, with lovely thatched roofs to shade you from the sun, a couple of chairs, and a little fridge where you could keep their expensive drinks cool. They even came and served you food. I approached the area and asked,

---

'Do you have any of those cabanas left?'

'Good news, yes, we do sir. I have one left.'

'Fantastic, I'll have it.'

'That'll be $690.'

> 'Oh no. Sorry, I don't want to take one home with me, I just want to rent it for the day.'
>
> 'That is the rental price, Sir. I only have one left, that'll be $690. Do you want it?'

I thought to myself, 'I can't justify that,' and walked away. But I went back fifteen minutes later because I couldn't take the risk that they would be all sold out.

Theme parks manage the four fundamentals brilliantly, so they can get every single dollar out of the customer – and the customer thanks them! Let's have a look at how they can charge just short of $700 for a day.

1. **Comparison:** First, let's look at the fundamental of comparison. Compared to the alternatives – not sitting, going round in circles on the rapids, lying on the ground in the baking sun, or going home and disappointing my son – $690 doesn't seem so bad.

2. **Value:** My boy Sean had looked at the park's website online before we came, and he could name all the rides and knew the ones he wanted to go on. There was one ride, a drop slide on top of the volcano, that he was desperate for us to ride because we could race each other. 7,500 visitors a day can't be wrong – there had to be some value in this water park.

3. **Scarcity:** We were in the pizza restaurant, buying their over-priced pizza and eating it standing up, with an over-priced coke, because there was nowhere to sit. This park had just opened, everyone wanted to visit,

but they only let 7,500 people in per day. How many cabanas do you think they had? Just thirty-eight! That's supply and demand in action.

4. **Urgency:** If I didn't take that cabana, guess what? It'll be gone. I needed to hire it quickly before the person behind me took it, or I expired from heat exhaustion. And you know what? When I went back 15 minutes later, it *was* gone.

If I was going back to Volcano Bay do you think I'd pre-book one of those cabanas? Probably. Do you think they'll have any trouble renting those cabanas? Probably not. As long as they keep the value high.

And that's how they get almost $700 out of people. Sean and I got on just five rides in total.

I want you to think about these four fundamentals when selling anything. In this book we're looking at the motor trade, but the fundamentals apply to any other industry. The four fundamentals have to be satisfied for someone to buy that big-ticket item. And if they're not satisfied, you're going to have a hard job selling.

·

TWO

Your Mindset Basics

In this section we're going to cover mindset. What is it that makes one person a great salesperson, while others really struggle? Are salespeople born, or made? When you get the mindset basics right – managing your own and understanding your customer's – the process runs smoothly.

Far too many people in sales have simply fallen into it. There's an old adage – if all else fails, try sales! If they can't flip a hamburger right at MacDonald's they go off and sell cars. Selling should be seen as a career – not an alternative to flipping burgers.

The poor salesperson lets their emotions lead the way. When they're down they take the customer down with them. They won't have a plan – they'll simply be driven by their own emotional roller-coaster. The poor salesperson thinks all customers are alike, blasts in with corny scripts and inappropriate reasons the car is right for the customer. They don't read the emotional signs, they chase the customer on their emotional journey and if they do make a sale, complain it wasn't big enough.

A successful salesperson has a business plan. They know what they need to do to make money and sell cars. A successful salesperson will be able to understand the customer's buying emotions, guide them on an emotional journey, satisfy the four fundamentals, develop rapport, manage their own emotions – and get the sale. A customer who has been well-handled on this journey will be a customer for life. The successful salesperson is sowing seeds for their future, and yours.

In this part of the book we'll look at the emotions involved in selling – both the salesperson's emotions, and the customer's.

The Customer's Emotional Journey

Think about how the average customer sees us as salespeople:

Figure 2.1 The poor salesperson triangle

Look at this triangle. The traditional, poor salesperson spends time at the top of the triangle, on the meet and greet, and qualifying a customer. He spends a bit of time presenting and demonstrating the product and the service. Then he spends all this time at the bottom of the triangle negotiating on the deal, the close, and the money. I think there's a huge problem with this, because the more time spent on the money and the deal, the more we're eroding the profit margin.

Why? Well, let's have a look at the customer's emotions on this graph:

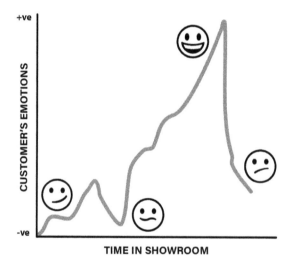

Figure 2.2 Customer's emotions graph

On the left we have the customer's negative and positive emotions. Along the bottom we have the time that they're in the business. Where do you think your customer's emotions are when they first enter the business? Negative or positive? While they might like the idea of a new kitchen or bathroom, a new car or a holiday, when they enter your business they're thinking about the buying process. When the average customer thinks of salespeople, do they feel positive or negative?

Look at this survey done recently by Reader's Digest:[1]

Australia's Most Trusted – Top Three

1. Paramedics

2. Fire-fighters

3. Pilots

They listed different professions in order of public opinion. Number one, right at the top, was ambulance drivers and paramedics. They save people's lives for a living! In the second spot were fire-fighters. Now, my wife likes fire-fighters but that's probably for a different reason! Number three in the list were pilots – highly professional in every way. Where do you think car salespeople come in that list of forty-five professions? Number forty-three.

At forty-four are the politicians and at forty-five we have direct and telesales people. These are the guys going door to door asking you to change your gas supplier or phoning you while you're eating dinner with the family to help you claim your PPI.

Who do you think was at number thirty-nine? Which profession just barely commands more respect from the general public than car salespeople?

39. Sex workers

40. Journalists

41. Taxi Drivers

42. Real estate agents

43. Car salesmen

---

1   www.smh.com.au/national/australias-most-trusted-sex-workers-trump-pollies-in-public-confidence-stakes-20110622-1ge82.html

In at number thirty-nine we have sex workers! Is it any wonder that customers come in with their hands deep in their pockets? That they walk right around the boundary walls, as far away as possible from the salespeople? Sometimes when you walk up to a customer, you can see the fear in their eyes, 'Just looking!' Of course, some customers will come in happily, chatting away, making eye contact, but often these will be the ones who don't buy, or if they do buy, we can't get them approved on finance.

We have a saying where I grew up in Australia – 'show or dough' – the people with the real dough (money) often don't show it, and those people flashing the bling-bling sometimes haven't got the dough. In my experience, the real customers are the ones that are standoffish, and come low down on this graph. Let's follow them through the process, their 'customer journey', and see how their emotions change. When the customer comes into your dealership, they will go all the way around the used cars first, even if they want to buy a new car. The customer's emotions might rise a little because they're thinking, 'Well, it's not like Dodgy Dave's down the road,' but then they see one of us salespeople heading towards them. Now their emotions do a sharp dive and they start getting their objections out: 'Just looking, early days.'

Then we go and do a proper meet and greet. We don't say, 'Can I help you? Are you alright there?' because that's what all the other salespeople have said to him. We do a nice meet and greet, something along the lines of: 'Hi, how are you? What brings you here today? Oh, you want to look at the Q5? There are 4 or 5 different models of Q5. Which one have you been researching online? Oh, the S-Line plus, what was it about the S-Line plus that put it on your shopping list?'

Early on in the conversation we might say, 'I'm sorry, I didn't even introduce myself. I'm Simon, and you are?' When the customer realises that there's no shark fin on our backs do you think their emotions might rise a touch? Probably. Then we can start qualifying the customer, not just the deal.

What's the difference between customer qualification and deal qualification? Deal qualification is the difference between three doors or five doors, petrol or diesel, manual or automatic. Customer qualification is: It's a Tuesday, are you on holiday? What do you do for a living to get a day off in the middle of the week? School teacher? Big kids or little kids? That's when we get to know the customer.

Needs or wants: Bluetooth, anyone?

Deal qualification is important, but we also have to qualify the customer's needs and wants, and I would argue there's a huge difference between what a customer needs, and what they want. Let me ask you a question: what's more important when you're selling a car, increasing the customer's needs, or increasing their wants? Needs *have* to be satisfied. If I only have one leg, I need an automatic. But if we all bought cars based only on needs we'd all be driving ten-year-old Skodas. We just need to get from A to B. I would suggest that most people change cars because of wants and desires.

Let's be silly for a second. Does anyone *need* leather interior in a car? Nope, not many people. I would suggest that's a *want*. However, if you try and sell a Range Rover Sport without leather interior, I think that would be quite difficult. Do you think they'd even build you one? Probably not. What about air conditioning in the UK? Is that a *need* or a *want*? Probably a *want*.

If you tried to sell me a car without Bluetooth, you'd have a fight on your hands. Under analysis, is Bluetooth truly a need or is it a want? It's probably a want, but I'd tell you I needed Bluetooth! Why? Because I love to listen to Australian music from Spotify. You don't get much Australian music on Radio Two in the UK, and I really want to listen to Spotify. I might tell you it's a need, but in reality, it's still a want.

It's important to distinguish between needs and wants, because people will spend the bare minimum satisfying their needs, but will spend extra money to satisfy their wants and desires. Look at the restaurant industry. There's only a certain number of calories we need to consume every day to survive. We go to a restaurant not because we *need* to survive, but because we *want* the experience, the ambiance, the conversation and a nice glass of wine. *We want more than what we need.*

That's why we qualify the customer's wants as well as their needs, and if we do that effectively, the customer's emotions might just come up.

Where are they now? The Kirstie & Phil...

What next? Where do we take the customer on their emotional journey? Years ago, we used to look at the customer's trade-in or part exchange after we'd done some presentation and demonstration. I suggest we use it early in the process as a qualifying tool.

We call this the 'Kirstie & Phil.' In the UK there's a house-buying television program called *Location, Location, Location*, and they always start off with the customer's current situation. Kirstie and Phil, the show's hosts, always start with something like this: 'Meet Frank and Mary, they currently live in the middle of London. They want to move out of London because of their son, young Johnny. There's no space for Johnny to kick the football around and Johnny wants to be a football star when he grows up. They want to move to the Aylesbury area with a bit more space. Frank will keep commuting into the middle of London. Mary wants to be the next Mary Berry, so ideally, she'd like an Aga, so she can do lots of baking. Frank plays the bass guitar and wants a man cave because he's been disturbing the neighbours.'

In the first minute of this TV programme they set up what the customer likes most about their current situation, what they don't like, and why they're looking to change.

We're going to do the same thing for a car customer. We're going to find out what they like most about their current car, what they don't like about their car and why they're looking to change. Simple!

In the rest of the program all Kirstie and Phil have to do is walk into a house and say, 'Hey, Mary have a look at this kitchen, you'll be cooking up a storm. Frank have a look at this for a man cave, you won't disturb anyone here. Now the compromise on this house is that the back garden's not that big.' Then at the next house, 'Have a look at the back garden, Johnny is going to love this. Have a look at the man cave. Now, Mary, the compromise on this house is that there's only a galley kitchen.' At the next house, 'Have a look at the football pitch, the huge kitchen and the man cave. The compromise on this house is that it's £80k more than what you want to spend.'

We need to look at the customer's current car early on in the process as a qualifying tool. People want to know what their car is worth, so work with the grain, not against it. Don't have a battle with the customer. When the customer feels like they're getting what they want, they're more likely to be receptive going forwards.

We're not going to give the customer a valuation on their car right away, because as soon as the customer has got the valuation they're going to leave. We do something called third party negotiation. We ask the customer, 'Would you like an idea of what your car is worth? Great, let me show you the **science** we're going to use to come up the best price. We're not just going to look on a website or some guide or pluck it out of the air. You tell me all the good things about your car, and I'm going to go and give it to my boss, John. Even though it's a car we might sell ourselves, what John will do is ring around some **independent buyers** to get the best money for your car.

'Effectively we'll do the shopping around for you. That's why we're one of the biggest dealers in the area. That's going to take twenty minutes or so, are you alright for time?' That's called setting the agenda, we're going to come back to that later, but we can see that the customer's emotions have risen. Because we found out their true needs and wants, we can use that information to go into the presentation of the new product or service. The customer's emotions will rise again.

Now we're going to demonstrate that new car. When they're taken for that drive they'll be thinking, 'Yeah, I love this, it's beautiful.' In their mind, ownership questions start kicking in. We can prompt mental ownership by asking questions like, 'You said you drive to London regularly, how long does it take you to get to London?' In the customer's mind they'll see themselves driving to London in their lovely new car.

Now we can ask a trial close question, where we separate the product or service from the money. If the product or the service isn't right, it doesn't matter how cheap it is. In the car world we say something simple like:

'Well, John and Mary, it's nice isn't it? So listen, if everything stacks up right is this the car you'd like to be driving for the next two or three years?' Or,

'Apart from the numbers side of it, is there anything stopping you from wanting to go ahead with this car?' Or,

'If we get all the figures right, is this the car for you?'

But the instant we ask any of those commitment types of questions what do you think starts happening to the customer's emotions? You're right, they start going down.

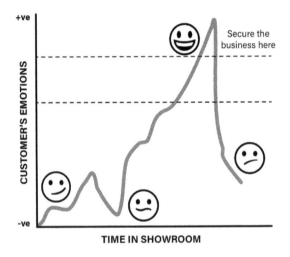

Figure 2.3 Customer's emotional journey

Look at the two lines on the graph. We need to close the customer before they get to the top line, to leverage maximum emotional advantage. In between these two lines we might close the customer, but we might sacrifice some profit. The only way we're ever going to close them below the bottom line is if we bought the business because they have cooled right down.

We have two sides to the brain, left and right. The right brain-left brain theory originated in the work of Roger W. Sperry, who was awarded the Nobel Prize in 1981. While studying the effects of epilepsy, Sperry discovered that cutting the corpus callosum (the structure that connects the two hemispheres of the brain) could reduce or eliminate seizures. However, these patients also experienced other symptoms after the communication pathway between the two sides of the brain was cut. For example, many split-brain patients found themselves unable to name objects that were processed by the right side of the brain but were able to name objects that were processed by the left side of the brain.

Based on this information, Sperry suggested 'one side of the brain deals with emotional thoughts, like love, respect, ego, fear, hurt, anger, etc. The other side of the brain deals with the analytical stuff, like gearing ratios, sets of accounts, analysing things, APRs. Generally speaking, the left side of the brain tends to control many aspects of language and logic, while the right side tends to handle spatial information and visual comprehension.

Now, like a lot of science stuff, this was only a hypothesis and has been disproved and disputed over the years, but it's still a really useful model. So, we're going to use it to help us think and talk about the customer's emotions.

Let's look at the emotions of the customer on this chart again, whenever we're talking about driving the car or them using it in their life, emotions come up. As soon as we talk about money and finances, we're forcing the customer to go into the analytical side of the brain, and that's where the emotions come down. The longer we're spending with the customer in the analytical side of the brain, the less profit we'll end up making. Let's go back and have a look at the triangle. The triangle is the wrong way around.

The PSP or the traditional salesperson is spending the least amount of time on the meet and greet, qualifying, and building rapport, and the most amount of time on the negotiation, the figures, the closing. Maybe that's why we get that bad reputation.

Let's flip the triangle over. Let's spend the same amount of time with the customer but spend the majority of the time at the top of the triangle on the meet and greet and qualifying, and use their car as a qualifying tool. Then when we spend the same amount of time on the presentation and the demonstration we can present the right features, to the right customer, at the right time. Then we can spend the least amount of time on the close.

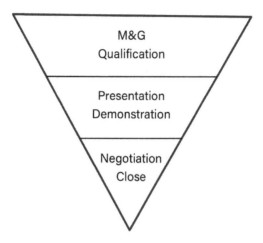

Figure 2.4 Good salesperson triangle

When you've been selling for a while, in any industry, when you come back from the presentation or demonstration of the product, and the customer's emotions are really high, and if you close those people within two minutes, isn't the profit in the deal usually pretty good? Aren't they easy people to deal with? Don't they buy other accessory products as well, nice and easily? These people are so nice they give you good Customer Satisfaction Index scores when your manufacturer asks how you dealt with them. They're the people, if there's a problem with a delivery time, that apologise to you for not calling in advance of their appointed time. They're the nice people to deal with.

The flip side? We come back from a demonstration drive and try to close, and five minutes go by. Then ten minutes, twenty minutes, you're like a yo-yo going back and forth to your manager. We're eroding our profit all the time. They're the customers who keep negotiating after the deal is done. If there's a problem with delivery, they're shouting, looking for reimbursement.

How do we avoid being a PSP? We must remember to spend more time opening people up and less on closing.

I was shown these two triangles by Tony Ireland when I was eighteen years old, and he said three things to me:

> 'Number one, Simon, you're going to remember these two triangles for the rest of your selling career.'

> 'Number two, they're going to make you a lot of money if you fully understand them.'

> 'Number three, do me a favour, make sure you teach someone else.'

He was right on all accounts – I have. And I've spent the last seventeen years of my life teaching other people too.

Whenever my sales have gone off and I look at what I'm doing wrong, it's because I'm spending more time on the negotiation of the close and I haven't spent enough time opening people up.

What's Your Sales Business Plan?

Now it's all well and good knowing how to navigate your customer around their emotional journey, but do you know how many customers you need to speak to to make a sale? Do you have sales goals and a plan? How do you know if you're doing the right things?

Let's say you want to sell 180 cars this year, that's the goal you set yourself. The average value of the cars is £15,000, which works out at 2.7 million pounds of turnover.

If you had your own coffee shop turning over 2.7 million pounds, would you have a business plan? You probably would.

Imagine the start of the financial year, going to your bank manager, and the bank manager asking how much coffee you're going to sell this year, and you say, 'I dunno, just as much as I can.' What do you think the bank manager would say? They'd want you to have a business plan, broken down, with how much coffee you expected to sell.

If you had your own business selling 2.7 million pounds worth of coffee would you insist your staff spoke to every customer, every time, with a big smile on their face?

Would you insist they upsold every customer, every single time?

Would you insist they knew why your coffee was better than Starbucks or Costa Coffee?

Of course you would.

Would you ask the customers to come back again? Would you thank them for their business? On the way to work would you go past your competitors to see what sort of loyalty program they had? You would! In a nutshell, you'd run it like a professional.

As a salesperson you *are* running your own business turning over 2.7 million pounds. Every top salesperson I've ever met always treats it as their own business, because you are running a business, *within* someone else's business.

Batting averages

I want to introduce Frank Bettger, who wrote a book in 1955 called *How I Raised Myself from Failure to Success in Selling.* Frank was struggling. As an insurance salesman, he thought selling was not for him after spending 10 months selling insurance without any real success. He went into the office to resign and collect his personal belongings and walked straight into the middle of a sales meeting. He didn't want to be rude, so he decided to wait to leave until it finished.

In the meeting the president of the company, Mr Walter Talbot, said: 'Gentleman, this business of selling narrows down to one thing, just one thing. *Seeing the people.* Show me any man of ordinary ability who will go out and earnestly tell his story to four or five people every day and I will show you a man who can't help making good.'

Frank thought that maybe his boss was right and decided to give it one more month. He was going to see the people.

Frank was also a baseball player, and every part of the game gets analysed. So, Frank started to apply the same analytical approach to selling. He's largely credited as the man who put science into selling. Some believe he's the man that came up with the sales activity funnel.

He started to keep records of the number of sales calls he was making. Over the next 12 months, he proved that his boss was right. Selling was a numbers game. Some will, some won't, so what, next! In that 12 months he made 1,849 sales calls to tell his story of life insurance. 828 people were interviewed or listened to his story and he was able to qualify them. 65 people said yes to his offer. But Frank did something else which has largely been forgotten – he took it back to how much each stage in the process was worth to him. Those sixty-five yeses made him $4251.81 in commission. Every time he made a sales call, it was worth $2.30. For Frank, what this meant was that each sales call was getting him closer to his goal. If people bought or didn't buy, if they slammed the door in his face, shouted at him to leave them alone, said they never buy at the doorstep, no matter what, in his mind Frank would say, 'Thanks for the $2.30.'

Frank made it into a business plan. If he wanted to earn $500 a month, he divided the $500 by $2.30 per door, which meant he had 217 doors to knock on each month. That's the activity he had to do to get the results he wanted.

Sales activity funnel

In the car industry our sales activity is increasingly starting with internet inquiries. From the internet enquiry we've got to get to a telephone conversation, which can sometimes be difficult, but we're going to show you some different ways to improve that. The whole idea of a telephone enquiry is to get people into the business. Let's call these people an Opportunity To Do Business – OTDB. In your dealership, you might have an OTDB log, frequently done electronically, but some people still do it on paper. From an OTDB we'll get a certain number of people through the process of being fully qualified.

Of course, ideally you'd like to get everyone's name, address and details, but in the real world some people are going to say, 'No, I'm just looking,' and we won't be able to open them up and get the details. From those qualified people a certain number will go for a demonstration drive. Are you going to get everyone into a demonstration drive? No. In fact, do you want to get everyone into a demonstration drive? If you've got that eighteen-year-old kid who wants to know how fast the car will go in reverse, you might want to speak to your management team first! Can you sell a car without a demonstration drive? Yeah, of course you can. But I'd argue, why bother? Because the demonstration drive is going to raise the desire in the customer, it will raise their emotions. More desire means more chance of closing that customer with more profit in the deal.

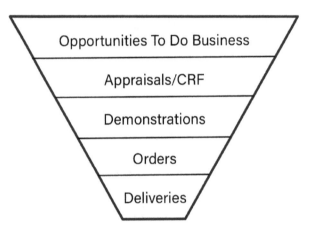

Figure 2.5 The sales activity funnel

From the demonstration drive we'll get a certain number of people who are sold – but even then, they might 'fall out of bed' because they can't get the finance approved. If we speak to 100 OTDB and that produces ten delivered units, when we want twenty delivered units, how many people would you have to put in at the top of the funnel? 200.

Does size really matter?

Let's compare salesperson A and salesperson B. Salesperson A speaks to 100 people, or 100 OTDB. He then gets 50 names and address details, fully qualified customers. He gets 40 bums in seats for a demonstration drive, and he sells and delivers ten units. Salesperson B, she speaks to 100 people, she gets 80 names and address details. She gets 20 bums on seats and sells and delivers ten. Here's a trick question for you, who's the best salesperson – A or B?

100	Opportunities To Do Business	100
50	Appraisals/CRF	80
40	Demonstrations	20
10	Orders	10
10	Deliveries	10

Figure 2.6 Sales activity funnel

They're both equally as good. Or equally as bad! They're both converting 100 OTDB into ten delivered units. They have different strengths and weaknesses, in different areas. Let's analyse it.

Salesperson A got 100 opportunities to do business, and from that he's got fifty name and address details. Could that be improved? Of course. From those fifty qualified customers he's got forty demonstration drives. That's pretty good, most people would be happy with that. But from forty people on demonstration drives he's only sold ten. Could that be improved? Definitely!

Here's another trick question for you – has salesperson A got an opening problem or a closing problem?

You might be thinking he has both and you'd be right, but I believe the closing problem stems from an opening problem. If only half the people will give him their name and address details, what are his rapport-building skills like? Is there any obligation built up? I'm going to be cheeky here for a second…

think back to your single days: it's like asking for a date before you did the ground work and chatting up! You might not get there, or if you did get there what's the quality of the deal like?

Let's have a look at salesperson B. She spoke to 100 people, got eighty name and address details. What do you think of that, pretty good isn't it? But from eighty qualified people she only got twenty bums in seats. Could that be improved? Of course. From twenty bums in seats she sold ten.

So, who is the best salesperson? Neither! They've just got different strengths and weaknesses.

What areas could salesperson B improve? I think she may be a cherry picker. Only taking people for a drive if she thinks she needs to in order to sell them a car. However, she may be missing out on a lot of deals. You see, she is selling 50% of the customers she is taking on a demonstration drive. But only 20% of her total OTDB are ending up on a demonstration drive. Or a 20% demonstration ratio. What do you think it should be?

Let's say she improves her demonstration ratio by just 10%. That would mean she would have demonstrated thirty customers as opposed to twenty, and based on her closing ratio of 50%, she would have sold fifteen cars as opposed to ten.

A 10% improvement at the beginning of her process has given her a 50% increase in results.

In which stage of the process are you most interested? If I gave you a magic wand and you could have as many people in any stage you wanted, where would you want the most people? I'd take delivered… 'show me the money!' So let's do what Frank did, and take it back to how much each stage in the process is worth to you.

Let's say you got £100 per sold car. That means both salespeople earn £1,000 commission for the ten units sold.

Let's look at salesperson A. Every time salesperson A had an OTDB, whether that person buys or doesn't buy, it's worth £10 to him. Every single time salesperson A gets a customer's name and address details, that's worth £20 to him. Every time he gets a customer into a demonstration drive, that's worth £25. Every time salesperson B speaks to someone it's worth £10. Every time she gets the customer's name and address details, it's £12.50, and every demonstration drive is worth £50.

For a downloadable spreadsheet with all of the maths done for you take a look at www.symcontraining.co.uk/bookresources

Work out how much each stage in the process is worth to you and it might help your motivation! Imagine it's Sunday afternoon, you're on lates and every person you've spoken to all week has turned to shite. You see some customers walk in; they're pacers, with their arms behind their backs. They've had all weekend to buy a car, and now they're here to wreck your evening. You've got to go out there motivated, enthusiastic, and you've got to want to help them buy a car. That can be difficult, I know. But if you think, 'Hold on, there's a tenner out there,' even if they're rude to you, in your mind you can say, 'Thanks for the £10. Next.'

Could we use this as a business plan? Let's work out what you want to earn over twelve-month period. If you want to earn £50,000, take away your basic wage, work out how much commission in total you need to earn, and divide that down into the number of cars that you need to sell. It will likely be 150 to 250 – work it out and from there figure out what activities you need to do to get results.

Drop us an email and we'll send you an Excel business plan to help you figure out how much each stage in the process is worth to you, and what activity you need to do to get to where you want.

I want you to come to work, not to wait – I want you to come to work with a plan. Come to work to work. When you have a plan, you'll know exactly what activity you need to do this week to achieve the results you need.

You might be thinking, 'Hold on Simon, that amount of people I need to speak to are not coming into the business.' Well, now you know how many prospects from your database you need to call. That'll tell you how many times you need to go into the service department and chat to those guys. Don't wait for your boss to come and bring the business to you. Work out what you need to do and go and do it yourself. We'll show you how to do that later in the book.

This simple business plan is one of the best things I've ever seen for developing the right attitude, because if you think you can – you can, and if you think you can't – you can't.

Let's look at attitude a bit more.

Attitude – Midas Versus Sadims

Let's take a look at the spiral effect of attitude. It goes all the way from positive right down to negative.

How do you feel on a Saturday morning when it's nine thirty and you've done your first deal, with full profit margin, and they've bought all your bolt-on products? What do you think your weekend sales are going to be like? Great, right? Is there a bit of a spring in your step? Doesn't it feel good?

So you might be in the middle of the spiral, but now you've got that spring in your step. Does that rub off on to the next customer? Of course!

You go and speak to the next customer, and you sell them a car and they say, 'I can't believe I bought a car today, I just wanted to get a brochure.' And in our mind we think, 'Yes, result!' Then you go and speak to the next customer and they start by saying, 'We're not buying today, you're the first place we have been.' And that goes in one ear and out the other and you put them through the process and end up selling them a car. Do you have even more of a spring in your step and find yourself moving even higher up the spiral? You feel invincible.

A customer comes in and asks for the ridiculous. 'I'm looking for an Audi Q7, but it must be a convertible, it's got to be electric, it's got to be pink with purple polka dots, and the last dealership said I've got a lot of CCJs.' I'm exaggerating here, however when you're on a role you seem to be able to sell to anyone.

Ker-ching!

This takes you right to the top of the spiral, and we call this the Midas touch, after the mythical Greek King, Midas – everything he touched turned to gold!

By the same token, what's it like when everyone you spoke to for the last week has turned to shite? You dust yourself off and go and speak to the next customer. You sell them a car, yes! But when they try to get approved on finance all you hear is hysterical laughter coming from the business manager's office because they've got a list of CCJs as long as their arm. And you find yourself spiralling down.

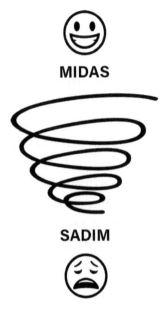

Figure 3.1 The attitude spiral

Don't worry, your business manager puts them up to a second-string finance company, Break Your Leg Finance. Break Your Leg Finance says, 'Hey, don't let that customer leave, they haven't finished paying for their last car. They haven't even *started* paying for their last car!'

You lose the deal. You spiral down even more.

You go and speak to the next customer and you sell them a car. Yes! Then your colleague comes in from his day off, 'Thanks for signing up Mr and Mrs Casey for me. Didn't they ask for me? It's my deal, because their next-door neighbour's postman came in for a brochure three years ago so it's definitely my deal, have a look at the diary.' And you lose that deal. You spiral down even lower.

You dust yourself off again and out you go. Thankfully you sell the next deal. But on the way home, the customer pops into a competitor who cuts the guts out of the deal. The customer is back on the phone, abusing you, and wants his deposit back. You lose that deal. Now you're right down at the bottom, where everything you touch turns to crap. The opposite of the Midas touch, spelled in reverse, Sadim.

When you're in the Sadims, how difficult is it to get yourself out? Salespeople tend to go into one of three modes:

Mode 1: Desperation. 'Hi, hello, how are you? Do you want to buy a car?' Does desperation mode ever work? No. The customer can smell the desperation. Remember your single days, out at a night club, looking for a date? If you were in desperation mode did it ever work out for you? No!

Mode 2: Woe is me. They put their hands deep in their pockets, they shuffle out to the customer, and the first meet and greet is just one word: 'Areyoualrightmate?' They follow that up with an inspired, 'Don't suppose you want to buy a car either? Us salespeople will be a thing of the past soon. You can buy cars from vending machines I've heard.' It's never the words – it's the way we come across to the customer.

Mode 3: Creative avoidance. Have you noticed that your colleagues (maybe you too), right when they *need* to speak to prospects to get sales, if they're in the Sadims, avoid speaking to customers? A customer comes in and salesperson number one, who's in Sadims, quickly picks up the phone and asks his wife what's for tea. Salesperson two has a sudden attack of diarrhoea and rushes off to find a toilet. Salesperson three does the long slow service walk, checks on that car that's being delivered in three weeks' time to see if the floor mats have been positioned well. Busy work.

We know the Sadims is just a cycle: we're going to have good weeks and bad weeks, good months and bad months. We need to remain consistent in that high level, not down on the Sadims.

Stop selling cars

The biggest fear when you're down in the Sadims is rejection. If you knew beyond a shadow of a doubt that the very next customer you spoke to was going to buy that car, that kitchen or that holiday home, you'd get out there and speak to them real quick. But what happens down in the Sadims is that the Dickhead Detector comes out.

A man in a business suit walks in on a Tuesday afternoon and you start thinking, 'Nah, they're just looking for the boss trying to sell him advertising space – dickhead!' Fifteen minutes later you see your colleague signing him up. Or, Saturday morning, you see a man with his son and the old Dickhead Detector comes out. They're just killing time while the wife is across the road shopping at Tesco – dickheads. Twenty minutes later you see another colleague signing them up.

We avoid customers because we're avoiding rejection. We all go through the Sadims at some point, and the top salespeople know how to get themselves out of the Sadims quickly. How do we get ourselves out of the Sadims and back in the Midases? Here's my advice – stop trying to sell cars!

I passionately believe that when we're in the Sadims, we try too hard.

I'm not a golfer, but it's one of those games I think I'd like to play. But the harder I try the worse I get. I grab that bat, grip it tight, and think 'I'm gonna hit this ball this time. I'm gonna hit it as hard as I can.' The harder I try the worse it gets, until I give up and think, 'You know what? Golf is not for me,' and then bang it goes straight!

I reckon it's the same in selling. The harder you try the worse it gets, and you fall into one of the three modes: desperation, woe is me, or creative avoidance. Here's my advice – stop selling cars and focus on the activity, not the results.

If you get the activity right the results will look after themselves.

If you're in the motor industry, I want you to double the length of the demonstration drive. I don't care how long your demonstration drive normally is, double it. It takes you out of that desperation zone.

I was at an automotive management conference recently, with around 2,000 people in the room, and I asked: 'Has anyone run out of fuel or broken down on a demonstration drive?' Half the room put their hands up. I asked them to leave their hands up if they sold the car. Three quarters of the people kept their hands in the air. Why? The car broke down and the closing ratio went through the roof. It's because you stopped talking about the car and started talking about them. You made a personal relationship with them, and it stopped you from asking the closing question too soon.

Now, I'm not suggesting you go off on a demonstration drive with a car with no fuel. But we can create the same result by doubling the length of the demonstration drive. You spend more time selling the product, raising the desire, before you ask for the business. Get the activity right and the results look after themselves.

Spread that enthusiasm

Does enthusiasm spread to other customers? Of course! People are always asking me how I stay so enthusiastic. Like everyone, some days I just don't feel enthusiastic, but I use a little trick that you might want to try: **Fake it till you make it.** Dale Carnegie said, 'Act enthusiastic and real enthusiasm will kick in.'

Did you ever play sport at school? Some days you just didn't feel like it. It was cold, wet and raining, and you just didn't feel like training. But your coach told you if you didn't get out and train today you wouldn't be on the team on Sunday. So you get out there, you start running around, two to five minutes in and you start feeling up for it.

At the moment I'm trying to lose some weight, because I have to iron my shirt over a wok to get the right shape. So, after making a thousand excuses I get on the treadmill, and something weird happens… for the first minute I want to die, the second minute I think I actually might die, but then between the third and fifth minute it doesn't feel too bad. Sometimes the days when I didn't feel like it at all end up being the best workouts I've ever had.

A little tip I learned many years ago: if you come to work and you don't feel like it, walk a touch faster. It sounds daft, but if you walk 25% faster more blood is going around your body and more oxygen gets to your brain, and you're going to feel better. Talk a touch louder. Enthusiastic people talk louder. You might also want to try talking a touch quicker.

Act enthusiastic and real enthusiasm will kick in. Remember, you can spread your enthusiasm to your customer. If you're not enthusiastic about your product or service, how can you expect your customers to be?

Be presentable

Do I really have to say this? All the other books and training courses will have told you this, but here we go: don't smoke, drink coffee, eat garlic or spinach and then breathe on your customer. Take a shower, comb your hair, get your clothes dry cleaned. Smile. Treat others how you want to be treated!

The Customer Has a Mindset Too!

We've looked at your mindset as a salesperson – now let's have a look at the customer's mindset. How much research do you think the average customer has done before they email, phone, or walk into a dealership? Motor industry statistics from Sophus3.com show that in 1995 the average customer physically visited *six* dealerships before they bought a car. A couple of decades later in 2015, and this reduced to less than *one and a half* visits. According to McKinsey & Company,[2] this figure has dropped to just *one* physical visit for some brands in some geographies. Are people shopping around less than they used to? No, they're just doing it all online.

---

2   https://www.mckinsey.com/industries/automotive-and-assembly/
    our-insights/innovating-automotive-retail

In their article,[3] Google broke the research into two parts. The first is awareness and consideration – the passive part of the research that can start up to eighteen months before people buy a new car. Since they're only passively looking, they might be driving down the road and see the new Peugeot and add it to their list to research. During that period the average customer visits seven automotive websites. They're not looking at specifications or pricing, they're just looking at photos and videos – it's still early in the process.

The next part of the research is when people are ready to buy. According to the National Automotive Dealers Association in America (NADA), this is just over three months before people buy a new car. The NADA tells us the average customer spends sixteen hours and forty-two minutes researching a new car. We all know how averages work – on average Bill Gates and I are both worth forty billion dollars. He's worth eighty billion so on average we're both worth forty billion. So, some customers are doing no research online, and some are doing over thirty hours of research. Is it any wonder they know more about that car than we do?

In fact, Google provided a detailed look into the buying journey of Stacy, a thirty-two-year-old mother of two. In a three-month period before buying her new car, she did 139 Google searches, looked at eighty-nine images and watched fourteen YouTube videos.[4] When I first heard how much research people are doing online in the motor industry, I was shocked – but maybe I should not have been.

---

3   https://www.thinkwithgoogle.com/marketing-resources/micro-moments/
    five-auto-shopping-moments-every-brand-must-own/
4   https://www.thinkwithgoogle.com/consumer-insights/
    consumer-car-buying-process-reveals-auto-marketing-opportunities/

When Emma and I were thinking about a one-week holiday to Gran Canaria, I noticed Emma on Google Street View, walking around the streets, virtually visiting a spa. She told me, 'You can't rely on the photos. I went online to have a sneaky look.' That research was for just one week of our life. Imagine how much time people spend looking at cars, which they'll have to live with for at least a few years. The cost of a week in Gran Canaria is a lot less than the cost of most cars. So of course people are going to do their sixteen hours and forty-two minutes of research online before they walk in the door.

Next, we are going to address how to approach that customer once they do walk in the door. The customer knows what they want, they've done their research, then they come into your dealership. Let's have a look at who you're going to meet.

Who you gonna meet?

All buyers are different, but there are some common characteristics. We need to ask questions to qualify the customer's buying emotions – and we have an acronym to help us:

S afety

P erformance/Practicality

A esthetics/Appearance

C omfort

E conomy

R eliability

Using SPACER we can determine the customer's buying emotion. We can use the situation around the last car I bought as an example – see if you can identify which emotion was more dominant for me. I last bought an Audi A6:

1. Was it safety? Possibly, I have two little boys, a wife and family I'm very fond of, but was that my dominant buying decision?

2. Performance? It was a three-litre diesel Quattro, so it's possible.

3. Practicality? Could be, I have a whole lot of things I need to put in the boot: from training material to courses, it's always full.

4. Aesthetics? It was an A6, Le Mans Sport, black edition with blacked out wheels and blacked out chrome… so you might say the aesthetics.

5. Comfort? I drive about 30,000 miles per year so comfort is really important to me.

6. Economy? With all the miles I do, diesel is really important.

7. Reliability? If I can't make it to a speaking gig, do you think the client would pay me?

You can see how easily we can convince ourselves that every customer is interested in every single aspect. That's one of the dangers with this acronym, SPACER. Often salespeople think the buyer will be interested in that product or service because of the things they are interested in themselves! Not necessarily true! You need to ask questions and find out what floats their boat.

Back to my buying emotions. If I was solely interested in reliability, I honestly wouldn't have bought an Audi product. I see the J.D. Power surveys, I know exactly where Audi comes in – I would buy a Honda or Lexus, because they always come in at the top. Reliability wasn't one of my dominant buying decisions. Economy? It was a diesel – a three-litre diesel – which ate tyres as if they were going out of fashion! Comfort? No, let me tell you the truth about a Le Mans Sport, the tyres are so thin I'm almost certain they paint them on, driving from London to Cheshire and I'd be crippled. They must take the suspension out and put steel rods in. It wasn't comfortable. Aesthetics? It looked like a pimp mobile! Safety? If safety of my family was my number one priority I'd be in a four-wheel drive vehicle. My boys are hardly ever in my car; if we go out as a family we go in Emma's car, a four-wheel drive!

The real reason I bought that car, which by the way was the wrong car for my job, is because the salesperson took me for a drive and I thought, 'Wow, I'm going to have a bit of fun. This is my mid-life crisis car.'

I traded that car and bought a two-litre diesel because the Audi A6 was the wrong car for me. My number one buying emotion for the two-litre diesel as opposed to the three-litre diesel? Economy.

We need to ask questions about the customer's current situation to find out what their buying emotion is. Don't focus on the performance of the car if they're a couple who have just had their first child and they're worried about safety and ISOfix child seats, and the practicality of getting a pushchair in the boot.

Don't sell what you're interested in. You've got to work out what *they're* interested in. You need to ask the questions to get the right buying motion.

Curry breath and cold hands

We also need to have a look at the customer's body language as a way to identify what type of customer they are when they walk in. While you may think you know all the signs and tells, we need to be careful when making judgments based on body language. Allan Pease[5], one of the best body language experts I've ever come across, talks about looking at *clusters* of gestures, because we can get it wrong if we focus on only one.

Some people think if a customer has his arms folded, they are standoffish, when in fact they might just be cold and trying to keep warm. If I'm talking and I cover my mouth you might think I'm telling a lie, when in fact I had a curry last night and I don't want to breathe all over you. That's why you shouldn't judge someone based on just one gesture.

Additionally, it's not just the body language that we need to look at, but the proximity as well – or the zones. How close we stand when we speak to people can have a huge impact.

Body language or circumstances?

Could a smile ever be aggressive? Let's say it's 11:30 at night, you're in the tube in London, in an empty carriage all by yourself. It stops at the next station and four youths get on wearing hoodies. They can sit wherever they want, they choose to sit opposite you. They look at you and smile. What's going through your mind now? Do you stay on? Do you get off? It might be the most innocent thing in the world, but now you can see how the circumstances around a gesture has huge impact on the feeling.

---

5   Allan Pease, Body Language, 1981

We operate on four zones of distance from other people:[6]

1. Public – 3.6m
2. Social – 1.2m
3. Personal – 56cm
4. Intimate – 15cm

Let's look at these zones in a bit more detail. The first one is the public zone which is 3.6 metres – we prefer to be 3.6m away from people to feel comfortable in Europe. Imagine you're on a beach in Spain on holiday with your family, and someone sits closers than 3.6m away: 'This is my piece of beach, go and get your own.'

What about when you're in a lift, if that 3.6m is encroached by complete strangers, how do you react? Often the barriers go up. As most people walk into a lift, they turn around to face the door, as our caveman instinct tells us to search for the exit; then we look up at the numbers or down at the floor until the lifts stops at our floor. If we're in a lift with a friend having a conversation and someone else enters, often the conversation will stop, and if it doesn't stop there's some sort of unwritten rule that mandates you talk in a whisper.

What do you think would happen if I entered a lift with three or four people inside, and instead of turning around and looking at the floor, I just faced them and smiled? It wouldn't matter which floor they were expecting to get off, they're all going to get off at the very next floor! They would likely be incredibly uncomfortable – I would've encroached on that 3.6m comfort zone.

---

6   Edward T Hall, www.study-body-language.com/Personal-distance.html

Imagine you go into one of these big shopping centres in the middle of town, like the ones my wife Emma loves, and there are two benches. On one bench you see someone sitting slap bang in the middle, claiming it all. On the other bench there's a guy sitting over on the left-hand side. Where will you go and sit? You'll go and sit on the right-hand side, as far away as possible from the other guy.

Guys who are reading this know it's no different when having a wee at the motorway services. You girls are lucky, you get a lovely little cubicle to go and do your business in, but us boys, we get a long trough. Guys will walk all the way to the end, as far away as possible, because we feel vulnerable when someone is standing behind us – especially when you have your willy in your hand! Blokes, think about it, what's it like when you're doing your business and someone comes and stands right beside you and strikes up a conversation? It's a bit weird! We need our 3.6m distance from strangers.

I've spent a lot of my life in aeroplanes. I even have my favourite seat – C3 – near the front, but not too near, so I can get on and off quickly, and I can use the loo easily. I regularly travel home on Friday evenings, but every now and then you get people who don't know the rules of an airliner. The rules are simple: everyone leans towards the window because that way we all get an armrest. Sometimes people sit right in the middle and take both the armrests. My only choice now is to lean to the outside and spend the whole flight getting bashed by the trolley. This is the 3.6m complete stranger zone in action.

The next zone is social, where we like to be about 1.2m away from people that we know socially. In a club, speaking to work colleagues, propping up the bar we might be 1.2m away from someone else. The question is, what do we need to know about someone to enable us to go from the public zone to the social zone? It's simple – their name.

Space invaders

The personal zone is 56cm. In the personal zone we speak to people about personal information. I see the personal zone being invaded all the time in car dealerships.

I hear salespeople ask the customer very personal information, such as how much money can they afford to spend, what their current car payments are, how much equity do they have. This is personal information, and if you haven't built enough rapport to allow you to go from the public, to the social, to the personal zone, the customer will shut down.

Then we have the intimate zone at fifteen centimetres. You shouldn't be at that stage selling cars! Intimate doesn't just mean a sexual relationship. You enter the intimate zone with your mum and dad, your children, or your partner when you give them a hug.

You've got to be careful, if you go to the next stage before you've got permission the barriers will go up. You've probably spoken to someone who is a space invader. They come and talk too close to you, and it doesn't feel right. You take a step back to be comfortable and they take a step forwards. You take another step back, and it ends up like a reverse waltz around the floor.

The zone distances we're talking about are for Europe, and these tend to be different in different parts of the world. What about Australians? There's a cliché that us Aussies are loud-mouths. I think there's a bit of truth in it! Australia is huge and there are only about twenty million people living there, and because of this all the spaces tend to be bigger and these zones tend to be bigger too. Hence, we talk louder to be heard.

There's a stereotype that Japanese people speak very quietly. I visited a town in Japan, a big old town with thirty-eight million people: Tokyo. The Japanese people were so nice, approaching my friend and I, getting very close to quietly ask if we'd like some saki. They felt comfortable that close, whereas we'd take a step back, because we felt uncomfortable.

Make sure you're not being a space invader to your customer. Don't encroach on their personal zones. When you ask for personal information, don't ask too quickly. Don't shout across the show room, asking your customer how much they can afford. In this situation the customer would prefer to be at the personal zone, and you're still dealing with them in the public zone.

Customer Types

We've looked at the customer's buying emotions, now we'll look at the customer's personality type. Of course, every customer is different and they behave in different ways, but we can draw some conclusions to help us make the sale.

You might have done psychometric profiles or some sort of personality test in the past, and they can be very revealing as to a person's character traits. However, we can't do personality tests when people are walking in the show room. Wouldn't it be nice to say to a customer as they walk in, 'Right, before we start talking about buying a car can you fill in all these questions, I'm going to do a DiSC profile on you.'

Let's have a look at where all these tests come from and then see how we can use them in the real world. William Moulton Marston,[7] a psychologist with a PhD. from Harvard University, wrote a book in 1928, *The Emotions of Normal People*, where he theorized that people's emotions could be categorized into four main types: Dominance, Inducement, Submission, and Compliance. Walter V Clarke, an industrial psychologist, was the first person to build an assessment tool, the personality profile, in 1948, based on Marston's four character traits. This theory of personality was further popularised by Catherine Cooke Briggs and her daughter Isabelle Briggs Myers, who eventually developed the Myers Briggs type indicator.[8] I can't keep up with how many of these personality tests are out there, but they all tend to come back to two main traits – a person's assertiveness and responsiveness to other people.

I'm going to take you through an oversimplified version, as it works a lot better in selling. Remember, it's not fair to put people into a box, we are all a combination of traits. When you do a psychometric profile, it will measure how much of each one of these traits you have. It can measure what you are really like inside, deep down, and how you portray yourself to colleagues at work and family at home.

Here's my oversimplified model with high or low assertiveness and high or low responsiveness to people:

---

7   https://discprofile.com/what-is-disc/history-of-disc/
8   http://blog.motivemetrics.com/A-History-of-Personality-Psychology-Part-1

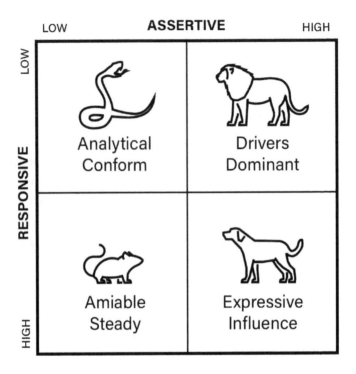

Figure 4.1 People-model

Let's take someone like Hitler. Do you think Hitler has high or low assertiveness? We don't know him, but let's imagine from what he's done, it's probably pretty high. What about his responsiveness to people? Was he more task or was he more people orientated? I would suggest he was more task orientated. On our matrix that would put him in the driver category.

Can you think of someone that you work with, a family member or a friend who is the driver or the director, task rather than people orientated? They're the drivers – we're going to call them the lions.

LION TRAIT

- 'Task' rather than 'people' orientated
- Decisive, determined and take control of situations
- Emotions are under control and they enjoy stable relationships
- Focus on being efficient and effective
- Frequently in a hurry, impatient
- Inflexible, poor listener and can be seen as stubborn

Lion type customers come in and go straight for the jugular, 'What's your best price on that? Right now? Cash, no part exchange.'

Lions

When lions come in, they tend to walk fast. Their conversations are often loud, direct, and to the point. They'll use words like best price, right now, cash, what can you do?

Their dress tends to be sharp. The lion might be the man that wants the Savile Row suit. He knows it's the best suit – not everyone else knows, but he knows. He might buy that Patek Philippe watch pre-owned by Eric Clapton; not everyone knows what it is, but he knows that it's one of only two that were ever made in the world. It's got nothing to do with money – it's a mentality.

The lions are the easiest to sell to. They might beat you up on the price but when they make the decision, it's made. Do they renege on their decision? No. They don't suffer from buyer's remorse.

One of our biggest clients is a lion. We've been doing training for them for the last twelve years. When I spoke to this man about what we were going to do for him and how we'd do it, the whole conversation lasted less than forty seconds. I started telling him about what we'd done for other clients and his exact words to me were, 'Simon, I don't care what you've done for other clients. What can you do for me? Just show me the results. I'll be happy to pay the bill.'

I want you to deal with the lion as a lion tamer does. The lion tamer doesn't go up to the lion and say, 'Here you go poor little pussy, what a lovely pussy cat.' Because the lion is going to eat you up and spit you out. The lion tamer doesn't go in and try to fight the lion, because if you fight the lion he's going to rip your head off, eat you up and spit you out.

DEALING WITH LIONS

- Plan to ask questions about and discuss specific actions and results
- Use facts and logic
- When necessary, disagree with facts rather than opinions
- Keep it business-like, efficient, and to the point
- Personal guarantees and testimonials are least effective – better to provide options and facts
- Do not invade their personal space

The lion tamer has the chair and the whip, and they're firm – so be firm right back.

Let's move on to the next group. Someone who is very high on the assertiveness and high on the responsiveness. These people are called the Expressives. People say that externally I come across as an expressive. The socialiser who's reactive and impulsive. Those people we call the puppy dogs.

PUPPY DOG TRAITS

- Reactive, impulsive, their decisions are spontaneous and intuitive

- They place more importance on relationships than tasks

- Emotionally expressive, sometimes dramatic, always enthusiastic

- With a short attention span they can be flexible, optimistic and risk takers

- Their talkative and gregarious nature means they can be persuasive

- Creative

We call them puppy dogs because what's a puppy dog looking for? Attention – a pat on the back. Look at what I do for a living. I'm writing this book because I want to help you and I want your adoration. For the puppy dog customers, we need to make them feel special.

Next we have the Amiables. Think about someone in your business, maybe a receptionist or someone in admin, someone who is nice, who is low on assertiveness but high on the responsiveness to people. An aside, just because someone's high on the responsiveness to people doesn't mean they're a nice person. A con artist would be very high on responsiveness to people, but he rips people off. Conversely someone might be very shy and might be the most generous person in the world, but they come across low on the responsiveness to people scale.

We call these people the mouse. The mouse comes in and is nervous to make a decision. So, what are mice like?

MOUSE TRAITS

- They can be dependent on others, not taking risks, but looking for security
- Respectful, willing, and agreeable, they are good group builders
- Emotionally expressive, they end up being everyone's friend
- Supportive and soft-hearted, they can be a little over-sensitive

Finally, we have people who are low on the assertiveness scale and low on the responsiveness scale, like my accountant. We call these people the Analyticals or Snakes.

SNAKE TRAITS

- They are co-operative, with a business-like precision in all they do
- Excellent at solving problems, they are motivated by logic and facts

- **They take time to make decisions, waiting for everything to be written down and detailed**

- **Low risk takers, they are sceptical, rational and critical**

A note about assertiveness. Frequently during training courses people say they want to be high on assertiveness because they'll be the best salespeople in the world. That's not necessarily true – some of the best salespeople I know are quite low on assertiveness, and we call them the smiling assassins.

So, we've got the lions, the puppy dogs, the snakes and the mice. Remember, this is an oversimplification, but it's a useful tool to help us work out:

1. How to identify that customer who's in front of you, and more importantly,

2. How to approach them.

Puppy Dogs

Puppy dogs come across similar to the lions – they walk fast and they tend to be loud. But their conversations are slightly different, not as direct and to the point as the lion. The puppy dog will want to talk more about you and the business, and will ask how everyone is.

Sometimes puppy dogs dress to impress. I have one client who's an extreme puppy dog – whenever we meet, he will say, 'Hello Mr B. How are you?' Then he takes my tie and turns it around to see what brand it is. The puppy dog is the man that might wear a Rolex watch and want to make sure you know it's a Rolex.

You might think that puppy dogs are easy to sell to, and you'd be right, but they take time. The puppy dog comes in on a busy Saturday morning and he'll introduce himself to you! He'll tell you he wants to look at the new Honda CRV because, 'I was driving down to Cornwall. Have you been down there this time of year? You should go, it's lovely before all the tourists get there. Anyway, I was driving down to Cornwall, and this car passed me, and I said to my wife, wow, that's the new Hyundai, and she said it's not. I said it is. She said it's not. I said it is! You know what, I had to prove her wrong, so I followed that car. It took me a good half an hour before I could catch him and guess what? There's a big H on the back of it, but it wasn't an H for Hyundai, it was the H of the Honda...'

And you're sat there thinking, 'Get on with it.' But if you cut the puppy dog off how does the puppy dog feel? Unloved. A puppy dog can be easy to sell to, but they do take time.

DEALING WITH PUPPY DOGS

- Seek opinions in an area you wish to develop to achieve mutual understanding
- Discussion should be people as well as fact orientated
- Keep summarising – work out specifics on points of agreement
- Try short, fast-moving experience stories
- Make sure to pin them down in friendly way
- Remember to discuss the future as well as the present

When selling to a puppy dog, metaphorically pat them, make them feel special: 'You're going to be one of the first people in the country with this new colour car.' Or, 'You've got the top of the range model, your colleagues at work won't have this one.' The puppy dog loves it.

Mice

The amiable mouse walks more slowly. They tend to speak quietly and dress conservatively. They tend to be less flashy. Sometimes they're apologetic in their approach. The mouse might want a quality watch, but he doesn't want a watch that's in anyone's face, and might choose an Omega, low key. When the mouse buys a suit, he'll be looking for Italian quality fabric, but buy it from Marks and Spencer. He wants quality, but not showy.

The mouse is either extremely easy or extremely hard to sell to, never in the middle. The mouse is nervous to make a decision. When you come back from a demonstration drive and you ask the mouse if everything stacks up right, or is this the car they want to own, they say, 'Oh yep. Yep, this is one for me.' But they won't tell you that deep down inside they're not sure of the car.

When you put a deal in front of a mouse and ask a closing question they'll say, 'I'm 99% sure that we're going to go ahead, but we just want to go across the road to Costa Coffee and have a bit of a natter. What time do you finish?' And you never hear from them again. You keep following up with them, but you can't get through to them, and eventually they leave a message for you with your receptionist: 'Can you tell your salesperson he was the best salesperson we've had. We really loved that Sportage, it was really nice, but we've actually bought a Hyundai i10.' The mouse was looking at a Sportage, but bought a small Hyundai!

The mouse is the person who didn't have the balls to tell you the car was too big or too small, because he didn't want to offend you.

So, be careful when dealing with a mouse. Don't go for what looks like an easy pushover. Don't allow the mouse to make too many choices. If you give them too many choices, they won't be able to decide at all. Tell the mouse how you're a family owned business, running for the last thirty years: 'Anyone could sell you one car, Mr Mouse. I don't want to do that, I want to sell you your next car, the one after that and all your family and friends' cars.' The mouse wants to know that you are in the top quartile for your Customer Satisfaction Index scores and how you're going to look after him, not just today, but forever.

DEALING WITH A MOUSE

- Work jointly, seek common ground
- Find out personal interests and about their family
- Be patient, avoid going for what looks like an easy pushover
- Use personal assurance and specific guarantees, and avoid options and probabilities
- Take time to be agreeable
- Focus discussion on how
- Demonstrate low risk solutions

Be careful of too many decisions. Think about how you'd catch a real mouse in your house. Could you ever catch a mouse by chasing it? No – you need to let the mouse come to you.

Snakes

The analytical snake, so called not because they're slimy and beady eyed, but because they analyse their prey. A snake has no teeth to rip the flesh off an animal, so it will only attack something when it knows it can win. The snake doesn't want to waste its energy or its venom attacking something it cannot eat, because if it attacks something too big it'll end up killing itself.

The snake as a customer is a man that comes in and asks you the question he knows the answer to. He'll ask about the fuel consumption, and when you respond, '38.9 mpg,' the snake says, 'It's 38.7!' And you're left thinking, 'Well, then why the fuck did you ask?' The snake asked to test you.

Snakes tend to walk slower. They are conservative dressers; their conversation tends to be detailed with figures and facts. They won't wear a watch, they can tell the time from their iPhone, so why bother! The analytical snake would go to Matalan, buy five suits and throw one away every three months. He's analysed the price versus performance of his clothes.

Are snakes easy to sell to? They can be the hardest ones to sell to because we're secondary in the buying decision. Even if they don't like you as a person, they might end up buying. You can tell a snake because they come in with the *What Car* magazine, with a target price. They have printed off all the information, sometimes they have a spreadsheet. They might say, 'I just need to get the dimensions for this car with one wing mirror folded in and the other one folded out. They don't have that in the brochure, they really should, shouldn't they?' And then they want to measure the length of the car even though all the dimensions are in the brochure. They just want to double check.

> ## DEALING WITH SNAKES
>
> - Use actions rather than words to demonstrate helpfulness and willingness
>
> - Stick to specifics – analytical individuals expect salespeople to overstate
>
> - Their decisions are based on facts and logic and they avoid risk
>
> - They can often be very co-operative, but established relationships take time

Questioning Techniques

To deal with a customer effectively and create a rapport, you need good questioning skills.

If building rapport with customers is something you struggle with, ask yourself a simple question: who is doing all the talking at the start of the sales process? If it's you, chances are you're not getting to know the customer properly. You're probably spending too much time talking about the deal, which makes it much harder to open your customers up and to get a fair profit out of them.

Think about it in terms of two famous TV interviewers. The first is Michael Parkinson: he's done some classic interviews – with Mohammed Ali, Billy Connolly or David Attenborough for instance – and ask yourself, how much talking does he actually do?

Then answer is not much. He's the master of the open question, which cannot be answered with a simple yes or no. He'll say something like, 'Well, David, you've been filming wildlife for the last sixty years, so tell me – what is it that still makes it fascinating to you?' Then he just sits back and listens.

Contrast that with the style of Jonathan Ross – it's much more about him than the person he's interviewing. Now I like Jonathan and I might have got it wrong here, but I doubt he will go down in history as one of the all-time great TV interviewers. But I think Michael Parkinson will, and that's who I want you to be with your customers.

So, ask open questions – *then shut up and listen.*

Let's have a look at some questioning techniques.

Open questions

Get your customers talking by asking the classic open-ended questions – who, what, when, where, why and how. Then listen to what they are telling you. Remember, open questions are just one part of the equation. It's actually the question *after* the initial question where you really get to know the customer. What I mean by that is, after you ask a customer a question, the follow up question is what really opens up the conversation:

'You're here on a Wednesday, what do you do for a living to get a day off in the middle of the week?'

'I'm a high school teacher and it's the holidays at the moment'

'Great, so what subjects do you teach?'

You don't need to know what that customer does for a living to sell them a car, however it will help build rapport. Or, try:

'How many miles a year do you drive?'

'About 20,000 or so.'

'Quite a lot then. Is it mostly for work or pleasure?'

'Mostly work.'

'Oh, what is it that you do for a living to do that many miles?'

We need to know about the product or service the customer is currently using, because if they like the reliability of their current car, isn't that what they're going to be looking for this time? If they like the roominess of it, they're going to want that again.

Ask what they don't like too. Is there anything they would change or improve? Anything lacking that they want on their new one? If they haven't got adaptive cruise control at the moment, that might be a sales point that's important to them.

We want to find out about their hobbies and interests – if they've got a towbar, what do they tow with it? If there's a football sticker on the back, who do they support? You might argue that you don't really need to know these things to sell your product or service – but it undoubtedly helps.

Ask them about their life. Use the customer qualification stage of the process to get to know them and build up a good rapport.

There are different types of qualifying questions. The key to asking qualifying questions is to make it conversational – no interrogations please. Use your computer tablet if you have one, or your Customer Requirements Form, but don't go through it line by line, as it's only going to put your customer off.

Get them to open up by probing them with simple questions like: 'Really, why's that?' And with the classic open questions – who, what, when, where, why and how – because they generally can't be answered with a blunt yes or no and that's what will open them up.

Closed questions

Closed questions are important too. We need them to close the sale. For example: 'Shall we go ahead with that?' They're not inherently bad, it's just open questions tend to be better suited to opening the customer up.

The key to being a good salesperson is not having the gift of gab, but the gift of listening. Listen to what's going to turn the customer on about your particular product or service, and it will help you to sell it to them.

'Alternatives' questions

These are where we give the customer two options:

'Are you calling from home or work?'

'Would you like to come in on Thursday, or would Friday be better?'

'Do you want tea or coffee?'

'Red wine, or do you prefer to drink white?'

If I simply asked you what type of drink you want, we could be here all day. But if I narrow it down to two choices, chances are they will probably pick one of them.

'Did you want to order that in the Iridescent Snowflake, or would the Postbox Red be better for you?' As a salesperson, you don't mind which one they choose – so long as they go ahead with the purchase.

These are great for controlling the sale, and we use them a lot in qualifying.

'Do you prefer three or five doors?'

'Petrol or diesel?'

But there is a danger: if you run too many together, it can sound like an interrogation, or 'speed qualification'. So, if you ask a customer if they prefer petrol or diesel, make sure you follow it up with: 'Tell me, why is that?'

Multiple questions

Streaming several questions together, or stacking multiple questions, is also a technique used frequently. For example, if I said to you: 'When you've finished reading this book do you want to download our worksheets or watch one of our training modules, or download all the modules so you can watch them this weekend?'

This might confuse you, because I've given you too many options. You have to be careful with multiple questions.

Salespeople tend to use them at one of two times – when they are speed-qualifying a customer: 'What are you looking for – petrol or diesel? Manual or automatic? New or used?' and it becomes an interrogation. Or, when they're nervous. Sometimes we don't even finish the sentence: 'Do you want to go ahead with that paint protection, or...?'

The trouble is, if we come across as nervous to the customer, it's the same body language signals as when someone is being shifty – and might have the effect of pushing them away.

Value-loaded questions

These can be effective, but again we have to be careful. A value-loaded question is where you put your own opinion into something.

'These seats are nice and comfortable, aren't they?' What if the customer says: 'I'm not that keen on them actually. I liked the seats in the other car we looked at.'? You can easily end up with egg on your face and no room to manoeuvre.

Only ask value-loaded questions if you are sure the answer is going to be yes.

Use the information you've gained in qualification and simply regurgitate what they've told you they like about the car. If they said they wanted the performance of a V8 engine, and that they loved it, you can then say: 'Tell you what, that power is really good, isn't it?'

Use value-loaded questions to get customers into that 'yes' frame of mind. Just make sure you know the answer first!

Reflective questions

With reflective questions, whatever question the customer asks me, all I'm going to do is repeat it back to them.

'Does it come with air conditioning?'

'So, air-con is important to you?'

Why would we use a reflective question in the sales process? Two reasons. First, to show that you are listening. 'So what you are saying is, fuel economy is important to you because you drive to Scotland three times a week. Is that right?'

They are also great for handling objections. As consumers we often find it hard to say yes or no without giving a reason. If you're ever stuck with an objection, try repeating the objection and then shutting up.

'Hold on, I need more than that for my trade-in.'

'You were hoping to get more for your car?'

'Yes, because I've just had it serviced and done this and done that to it.'

The customer will explain to you why, and this gives you time to think of the right approach in addressing it. Even so, a funny thing often happens when you repeat and shut up to objections – sometimes customers will talk themselves out of it, without you saying anything.

> 'That red colour's not really grabbing me.'
>
> **'Even if everything else stacked up right, you're not sure if you could live with the red?'**
>
> 'Well... it depends on how it all stacked up. I suppose we could, we've had red in the past, it's quite a safe colour I suppose. What do you mean by "if everything stacks up right"?'

The probe

This one is more of a probe than a question. More accurately, it's a statement we cut off halfway through and allow the customer to finish.

For instance, if you want their phone number, you could just say: 'Can I have your phone number, please?' and you'll get either a yes or no answer, as this is a closed question.

Or, you could try the 'alternatives' route: 'Hey, where are you calling from, home or work? OK, and your number there is...?' And the customer finishes it off. This is the probe.

'OK so your postcode there would be...?'

'Your best daytime contact number would be 07...?'

It's a great way of getting information from a customer, without directly asking them.

Final thoughts on questions

We all *think* we know how to use open questions and that we're good at it, but I find thinking like a child will help you be a better questioner.

Think about when you were little. As kids we naturally ask open, inquisitive questions all the time. 'How much further?' 'When are we going to be there?' 'But why?' And for sanity, as parents, we say: 'Just because!' Open questions are almost knocked out of us.

If I took my four-year-old into a sweetshop and asked him what he wants, we'd be there all day. So instead I ask him: 'Do you want this one, yes or no?' 'Do you want that one?'

By the time we reach school age, it's all about closed questions. Everything is either right or wrong. As a society, closed questions are drummed into us.

Yes, we have to ask closed questions sometimes. But when you are qualifying customers, who is doing most of the talking? If it's you then you are probably asking too many closed questions. So work on opening them up. Practise open questions in your home and social life. Be a little childlike in your curiosity and inquisitiveness.

We Still Need Humans:
Us First, Product Second, Deal Third

Salespeople often ask me for ideas on how to close customers, and in particular how to close them faster. My answer is always the same. You can't close someone unless you've already opened them up.

There are three 'sales' we need to make before we can actually sell any product or service. We need to sell ourselves first, the product or service second, and then finally the deal. Where a lot of salespeople go wrong is that they try and sell the deal first, the deal second, and the deal third.

This might work if your prices are cheaper than everyone else's (remember the fundamental of comparison), but most salespeople would immediately become more successful if they would only go back to selling themselves first, before they start discussing the product, the price, or the cost to change.

Remember the triangle?

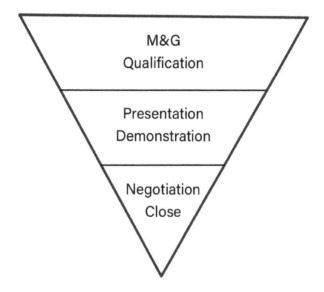

We need to spend more time on opening up the customer, and less time on closing them. Remember this throughout your selling career. There are always three sales in any sale. You have to sell yourself first, the product second, and then the deal.

Can you imagine going out to buy a suit and the sales assistant was rude and said something along the lines of, 'It's really close to closing time, you're going to have to come back tomorrow,' how many of us wouldn't go back to that shop?

You have to sell yourself first. Then you have to sell the product. If the suit shop only had pink and purple polka dot suits, would it matter how cheap it was? Probably not. We need to sell the product second and then we need to sell the deal last. If they don't like you or the product, it's always going to be an uphill struggle.

PART TWO

THE ROAD TO A SALE – PROVEN SALES WORD TRACKS

THREE

You Don't Need A Script

The nature of my work as a sales trainer means I spend a lot of time in airports, motorway services, and train stations all over the world. And, like you perhaps, I find myself drawn towards the bookstands that abound, and the 'success books' in particular – success in life, in business, and in sales.

Most of the 'success in life' books that I've come across tend to run along similar lines – build a core set of values and beliefs, focus on them, work hard, don't give up and so on. All very good stuff, however success in the financial sense often comes back to one thing… sales! More sales means more success!

When we look at the sales success books, they often tell us that we have to open the customer up, build their desire for our product or service, test their commitment with trial close questions, overcome objections, negotiate a price, and then finally close the sale. That's all good and inspirational, but isn't it essentially the same old same old? What I think is missing, and what I am constantly looking for, are the actual words that we use to connect with and influence our customers. The words that work in the real world. Isn't that what selling is all about?

When you started your career in sales, you probably learned quite a lot just by listening to your colleagues and adapting the words and the phrases that they used. In this next section we're going to look at the words that work. But a warning – scripts don't work.

Why Scripts Don't Work

Sales scripts don't work because the customer hasn't been sent their lines in advance!

Many sales trainers say that every great movie has a script – so if it works for the movies, it should work for salespeople too. While it doesn't sound 'scripted' when Harrison Ford or Meryl Streep is acting their part, they have an unfair advantage over your typical professional salesperson in that they are working with people who also have a script. In the real world, we are dealing with customers who can go off on any kind of tangent at any time.

Actors have another advantage over us as well, they can turn around at any time and say: 'Cut! Can we start again because I went off track there?' In a sales environment we can't do that. We can't say: 'Sorry Mr Customer, I got that bit of the meet and greet wrong, would you mind leaving and coming back in again?'

But here's the real reason why sticking to a script is a bad idea. If it really was that easy to take someone else's words and make them sound natural, the top actors wouldn't be getting paid millions of dollars per movie. The truth is, it's incredibly hard to do, and that's why I would urge you not to simply use the word tracks in this book word-for-word.

Instead, think of them as a framework for you to inject your own ideas and personality. Don't simply repeat them word-for-word. Take the fundamental concept and the meaning, twist it and change it, and make it your own. Then practise, practise, practise until you are comfortable with them. Don't try these word tracks out on real live customers until you are happy with the way they sound to you.

And if one track doesn't work for you, don't worry. There is no single technique that is guaranteed to succeed for everyone. There are some that I wouldn't use myself. But who am I to say they won't work for you? They have all been used successfully by some very successful salespeople.

These tracks can be used to sell any high value ticket items – from boats to bungalows, mansions to motorcars. Most of the examples I give you relate to cars and the automotive industry, but I've included a few yachts and houses to show you how flexible the tracks are. Once you have the tracks stored in memory, you can use them to sell anything.

Five Killer Phrases to Add to Your Process That Will Make You Money Today

We as humans are designed to copy other people. Sometimes this is referred to as the sheep mentality, or more politely as social proof.[1] Back in the caveman days we wanted to be

---

[1] https://www.psychologicalscience.org/news/releases/following-the-crowd-brain-images-offer-clues-to-how-and-why-we-conform.html

part of, and not away from, the group. There was safety in numbers. If we were by ourselves a sabre tooth tiger might come and kill us. In the group we can rely on the skills of the whole group for survival. So, from a very early age we are designed to copy other people. We'd like to think that's not the case, but let me try and prove it to you.

Have you heard a famous toothbrush manufacture say, 'four out of five dentists recommend Oral B'? If four out of five *experts* recommended Oral B and it's good enough for them, it must be good enough for me. In this example, if the vast majority of people recommended that brand, it must have been good enough for them – so it *should* be good enough for me.

Now if I said, 'I'm the best sales trainer in the world,' you might think (and rightly so), 'Who the hell do you think you are?' However, if I said *Richard Branson* said I was the best sales trainer he has ever met, would you believe him? Which one has more credibility?

Try typing into Google 'people standing and sitting social experiment' and you will see a video of a bizarre experiment where a lady in an optometrist waiting room stands up every time a bell rings... just because everyone else is. After this I bet you will end up on a YouTube spiral of people following the crowd. Derek Silvers will show you a video on his award-winning TED talk of people rushing to join a crowd dancing at a music festival. And one of the simplest examples of social proof is a group of four psychology students stopping and standing to look at the top of a building edge. If one person was looking at the top of a building, I bet not too many people would take notice. However, when four people stop and stare there must be something to look at.

So, if we know we are designed to follow other people to some extent, we could use phrases like:

Everybody Knows...

Everyone tells me...

Most of my customers...

Everyone I speak to...

There is an old saying...

If we imply that everyone else does something, maybe you should as well.

Let's look how we could use these phrases in selling. Let's say you are selling paint and fabric protection to a customer, and ask them: 'Do you have a paint and fabric protection certificate?' and the answer is a yes or a no. You haven't implied that most people have it.

Instead try the phrase: 'Do you have *your* paint and fabric protection certificate?' or, '*Where* is your paint and fabric protection certificate?' This approach implies that everyone has a paint and fabric protection, and you should as well. Then, when we introduce the product later in the sale, we have already conditioned the customer that most people take the product – and if it's good enough for most people it *should* be good enough for them.

If you are selling GAP insurance your initial hook could be, 'What level of GAP insurance do you have?' This implies that everyone has GAP insurance. When the customer replies, 'What's that?' or 'I'm not sure,' you can follow up with: 'That is something *most of our customers* have, because *everyone knows* that insurance companies can be hard work in the event of a total loss. *Everyone I have spoken to* who has had to deal with an insurance company loss adjuster says that they try and give you as little as they can get away with. That is why *most people* protect themselves with GAP insurance. *There's an old saying* that insurance companies love taking the money, but they hate paying it back out.'

In the real world you will only have to pepper the five key phrases throughout your presentation. However, you can see how these phrases use social proof to influence the customer to the advantages of GAP insurance.

The phrase, 'there is an old saying' works really well because the subconscious mind thinks if it's an old saying, it must be that way because it's been used for a long time – and if it's been used for a long time by a lot of people, it must be true!

How To Use The Sales Word Tracks

There are probably four different types of salesperson.

1. First there are the enthusiasts, who are so passionate about what their product or service can do for the customer that if you cut into them, it would probably say the company name right through their core. Apple employees, for example.

2. Then there are the process-driven types. They follow the same path every time, almost like a machine. If you listened to all their sales presentations back to back, they would all sound like a carbon copy.

3. The crunchers are the most assertive of the lot. They are the salespeople who just say, 'Do you want it? You said you like it, what's stopping you going ahead

with it?' When a customer starts to waver, they will confront them: 'You don't want to go ahead? But you said out there you wanted it! What's the problem?'

4. Finally, there are the personality salespeople. They sell themselves very well and customers buy into them. Their customers tend to buy whatever brand of product they are selling.

Which of these four styles do you think is the best? A trick question, as none of them are. They can all be successful. There's no right or wrong here, they're just different. It's the same with the word tracks in this book. If you come across a word track that you don't like, simply move on to the next one and see if it's better suited to your own personal style, or the industry you work in.

Please, do give them a try before you dismiss them. You may not feel comfortable saying a track to start with. In fact, you probably won't, because it's different to what you're currently doing. But if you were happy with the results you were getting, you wouldn't be reading this book. You have probably already recognised that you need to change the way you do things in order to improve the results you're getting.

FOUR

You Need A Process

Why do you need a process, and what is it? You need a destination (goal) and waypoints (steps). Your destination and waypoints were defined in the chapter where we looked at the numbers and determined your business plan. You know how many opportunities to do business (OTDB) you need to produce the number of delivered units you require, so you know how many people you need to put in at the top of the funnel.

Most people I know set goals. Lose weight, get fit, stop smoking, make more sales. I think that's great, I have even set myself some of those types of goals in the past. However, what I've found, and you might have too, is that some types of goals are better than others.

Dr Art Markman, in his book, *Smart Change*, differentiates between *outcome goals* and *process goals*. He claims that 'the most typical goal people pursue is an *outcome goal*. It refers to a specific state that you hope to reach in the future (like being a thin mother-of-the-bride). The second type of goal is a *process goal* that focuses on a set of actions you can perform. As a side effect of those actions, you may achieve some desirable outcomes, but your focus is on the actions, not the outcome.'

Have a think about the goals you've set recently. Were they outcome or process goals? Were you focusing on the end result or how to get there? How successful were you in achieving that goal?

There are a few reasons why outcome goals are bad news for salespeople (and everyone!):

1. You can't control the outcome. You can't *make* a person buy from you. Well, I suppose you could if you kidnapped their kid and held them to ransom, but you get the point. You can only control what *you* do.

2. If you hit roadblocks (and you will) you might feel disheartened – and with an outcome goal you might just give up, thinking you'll never get there. With a process goal, you just make the next call. Remember our friend Frank, and his batting averages? You know that every 'failure' is just a step on the way to success.

3. Comparing your outcome on a specific day to another person might make you feel like shite. But you don't know how many crap days they've had before. Comparing your actions to your own process goals can make you feel exhilarated as you can see your progress, step-by-step, day-by-day.

4. When you get stuck in the Sadims thinking about an outcome goal you've missed, your thinking can only

spiral downwards as you head towards one of the three modes: desperation, woe is me, or creative avoidance. When you stop 'selling cars' (outcome) and focus on the activity (process) not the results, the results will look after themselves.

You are probably agreeing with me now, because *everybody knows* that outcome goals are crap. *Everyone tells me* that they do much better when they focus on process goals. *Most of my sales training customers* get excited when I show them how focusing on process can help their salespeople stay motivated and make more sales. *Everyone I speak to* who has changed over to process goals says it's working for them. *There is an old saying,* frequently attributed to Gandhi: 'Sow an act, reap a habit; sow a habit and reap a character; sow a character and reap a destiny.'

Do you see what I did there?

Now, let's break down the waypoints, or the process, for moving us closer to our goal.

The Four Waypoints and How to Get to Your Destination Fast!

When I first started selling cars, my job as a salesperson was almost like a teacher. Customers would come in and say, 'Tell me about this model, tell me about that model.' Now more and more customers know what they want before they even walk through the door.

The modern sales process means people have done sixteen hours and forty-two minutes of research online before the walked in to your dealership. In fact, these days they don't start by walking in at all. Often the initial contact with the customer is through an email enquiry. Our job is to take the email enquiry to a telephone call where we actually speak to the person. From the telephone enquiry we need to aim for the appointment where people turn up and we can get a bum in a seat and raise the desire. From there we want to sell a car. If we can't sell them the car, we need to follow them up. Simple. So, where does it all go wrong?

With the incoming email enquiry, I've seen plenty of salespeople respond with: 'Yes, it's available, give me a call.'

Think this through – if they wanted to call you they would have. We need to engage with the customer. We need to give the customer a *reason* why they want to speak to us. Let's have a look at the four reasons why anyone is going to go to a dealership.

Four reasons buyers contact you

Imagine you wanted to buy a laptop. There are only four reasons you might go to one specific laptop retailer as opposed to another:

1. **Stock.** You pop into a shop called 'Laptops R Us' that's got every laptop under the sun, or they've got the latest Mac laptop and no one else has got it. Stock can be split in two: a range of stock or a specific item.

2. **Price.** We can't stick our heads in the sand – people will go to a particular retailer because of price. If that laptop was £1,000 everywhere else but one retailer had it at £800, which would you go to? Probably the £800 retailer.

3. **Location.** If you're living in London and that laptop is £1,000 everywhere except one retailer in Aberdeen who

has it for £800, would you drive to Aberdeen to save £200? It would probably cost £100 in fuel (especially if I blasted up there in that mid-life crisis Audi I accidentally bought). Probably not a good idea.

Price and location are linked. Flip it around. Everyone near you has the laptop for £1,000 but the Aberdeen retailer has it for £200 – who's driving to Aberdeen now? Or, do you think the customer might take that price information and go into a retailer in London and negotiate a better deal?

4. **You.** Let's say we speak to Jenny at 'Laptops R Us' over the phone, and Jenny seems to know what she's talking about. She asked some great questions about what applications we're using, she confirmed she had the Mac in stock, and also told us there was another option, a Hewlett Packard. She offered to set them up for us so we could take a look for ourselves if we came into the retailer. Stock, price, location, and you!

Let's have a look how this works in the dealership model by examining each of the waypoints through which we can connect with our customers.

FIVE

Waypoint 1: Email

Nothing's Changed, but Everything's Changed

Do you remember the size of the Yellow Pages when you were a kid? Every year a new copy would find its way to your house and thump down on the door mat. Thousands of pages filled with small type adverts for all sorts of businesses in the local area. If you wanted a car dealership, you'd flip to the car section and make your selection. How thick is the Yellow Pages now? Do they still even print the Yellow Pages?

These days we all start our research online. In the Customer Mindset section we learned from Google that customer research can be broken down into two parts: awareness and consideration, when the customer is passively looking; and then when they are ready to buy.

How much research does the average customer do before they email, phone or walk into their first dealership? How many websites have they looked at? How many emails have they sent out? Don't worry about the actual number – it's LOTS! In this first waypoint we're going to look at how to deal with incoming emails to your business and how to spot if the customer is in passive mode – and if they are, how to get them actively interested in your dealership.

We know we need to take the email inquiry into a telephone conversation – but first I have a little homework for you to do.

Email homework

Send an email to a few dealerships, your competitors, about the same type of car that you're selling, and write them an email along the lines of: 'Hi, can you tell me, is that car available and if so what's your best price?'

I promise you'll be shocked at the response you get. The vast majority of times when we do this exercise, I get comments like: 'Yes, the car is available, please call me,' or, 'If you want to know more details, call me.'

Salespeople say, 'Call me, call me, call me!' but we know that if the customer wanted to call us, they would have! We need to engage with the customer and give them a *reason* to call us.

As a reminder, there are three sales that happen in any sale: you need to sell yourself first, the product second, and then the deal. The following word tracks are designed to sell you first. They are designed to generate a *reason* for the customer to give you their phone number or call you, and get them to Waypoint 2.

When you get an incoming email enquiry you need to respond fast. Your speed of response needs to be less than one hour!

Why? Because they haven't just emailed you, they've emailed another four or five dealerships as well.

These word tracks should **not** be copied and pasted and sent as they are. They need to be personalised for each enquiry. What happens if you copy and paste? The customer could end up with nearly identical responses from each dealership! Sell yourself first, be personal, and thank the customer for the enquiry!

How much is my car worth? They want you to guess...

Let's start with one of the hardest email enquiries: 'What's my car worth?' If you tell the customer what their car's worth, do you think you'll ever hear from him again? Probably not. If you don't tell them what their car is worth will you ever hear from them again? Probably not. You're damned if you do, and damned if you don't.

You might want to try something like this:

Personalise and thank the customer for the enquiry!

The trouble with pricing a car without seeing it is it's going to be a guess – and I will end up guessing too high or too low. If I guess too high you would be upset if we couldn't give you that figure when we see your car. If I guess too low, we probably won't meet each other.

However, if it's a rough idea you need there are plenty of web sites like webuyanycar.com who will give a ballpark figure, we are normally a touch higher as they usually knock the price down when you go to their drop-in centres. I don't work that way.

If you want a more accurate figure from me without seeing the car, would you be able to give me a call while walking around your car? This way we will be able to get a more detailed description to get the very best price for you.

When is the best time for me to arrange a telephone appointment so I can ensure my sales manager is available for us to get you the best price on your car?

Many thanks for your enquiry,

Simon

You might be thinking it sounds mad to send the customer to our competition, webuyanycar.com.

If people have done sixteen hours and forty-two minutes of research online before they email, phone, or walk into a dealership they've probably already been to webuyanycar.com. It pops up as a Google Advert when you search for cars! So, if you tell the customer they can get useful pricing information from webuyanycar.com and they've been there anyway, you're not trying to sell. What does the customer think of you now? Trustworthy? Honest? Will they start to like you? Will they want to come to you rather than somewhere else?

Groundwork: reg #, address (check for location)

Now let's have a look at the second email we can send to the customer on 'What's my car worth?' I used to think I had to put everything in my first email and hopefully the customer would pick up the phone and speak to me or just turn up, but it doesn't work that way. If they wanted to call you, they would have. We need to *engage* with the customer, create a conversation – they say something, you say something. When you look at your WhatsApp messages or text messages with your family or friends you'll see a backwards/forwards flow of information – not a monologue, but a dialogue. That's what we want with the customer.

Here's the second email you would send to a 'What's my car worth?' enquirer.

Thank you for confirming that time.

Please could you email me the registration number of your car and the post code of where the car is registered to?

This will help me do a bit of ground work on your car before we talk on the phone. It will also enable us to get you the best price if you have the following items on hand;

- Service history and any invoices you may have for the car, and if the next service is paid for

- MOT certificate

- V5 registration document / log book

- Current finance settlement figure / Current GMFV

- Your Paint and Fabric protection certificate

What is the best phone number to contact you on?

Many thanks,

Simon

There are a few things in this email that might help create urgency because people might want to change their car before the next service comes up, especially if it isn't paid for. There might also be a hook for a service plan if you're selling them.

By encouraging the customer to get their MOT, NCT or Road Worthy certificate out, when you call them you can ask them; 'Mr or Ms Customer, do you have your MOT certificate on hand? Great, on the right-hand side there's a box called 'advisories' – are there any advisories you haven't had a chance to do anything about?' This is another way of creating urgency, because some people will want to change the car before the NCT test comes up.

By asking them to get their finance agreement ready, we are also assuming they will need or want to finance. We're not going to ask the customer: 'Do you owe any money on the car?' or 'How do you want to fund your new car?' We know most people borrow money for a new car, so let's just go down the assumptive route and ask people how many payments they have left or when is the GMFV due. Some customers might ask you what the GMFV is, and that gives you the opportunity to *engage* with the customer and explain that it's the Guaranteed Minimum Future Value.

The last item, 'your paint and fabric protection certificate' frequently results in a response, 'What's the paint and fabric certificate?' and gives you the opportunity to send them a video on your paint and fabric protection product, sowing the seeds early on.

What's the best price?

'What's your best price?' is the email we most frequently receive. So, how do you respond? Start off by personalising it and thanking the customer for the inquiry.

Someone who works for us tells a great story about a man called Peter. Peter was going to buy a television. He'd done all his research online and decided he wanted to buy a Sony Bravia TV. He went to the local retailer to have a look at the Sony and the sales guy said: 'Sure, I could show you the Sony, but I think you'd like to know that there's a new Panasonic TV. It's just being launched and for the same money it's got better smart functions, better resolution, better this…' and the salesperson got really excited about the Panasonic TV. But Peter hadn't done any research on the Panasonic and now he felt confused, so he said the only thing he could as a customer in that situation, 'Well thank you very much, I just need to go and think about it,' so he could go and do his research on the Panasonic.

He left that electrical retailer and he went into another one since he still hadn't seen the Sony Bravo yet. The sales guy there said, 'Excellent choice of TV. That's the TV I'd buy if I was buying a TV.'

Where did Peter buy the TV from? The second retailer of course. The second salesperson almost congratulated Peter on the amount of research he had done – and that's one way to personalise the email. Let's use our email sales track to see how to do it.

> **Personalise and thank the customer for the enquiry!**
>
> That car's in great condition. I brought it in for a trade-in myself from a lovely couple who are emigrating to Canada — that's why the mileage on the car is only 16,000km.
>
> Getting the price right is the easiest part of my job because we are part of the Symco Group, and we are one of the biggest internet retailers in the Mazda Network.
>
> The best price will be the amount of money coming out of your pocket, so we need to get the details about your part exchange to get you the best balance to change and monthly payments.
>
> Could I have the registration number of the car you are looking to part exchange please?
>
> Many thanks,
>
> Simon

By mentioning the 16,000km on the clock you make the customer feel good about the research he's done.

We ask for a registration number of their part exchange to bring the customer's attention to the importance of how much they'll be getting for their car too. When they give you the registration number, they'll also ask: 'What's it worth?' Now you can go back to the first track and say:

> The trouble with pricing a car without seeing it is it's going to be a guess – and I will end up guessing too high or too low. If I guess too high you would be upset if we couldn't give you that figure when we see your car. If I guess too low, we probably won't meet each other.

Some people will say they don't have a part exchange, and again ask for your best price, so let's try this approach:

> ### Personalise and thank the customer for the enquiry!
>
> That car's in great condition – I brought it in for a part exchange myself from a lovely couple who are downsizing their family home, and no longer need all those seats.
>
> We are one of the biggest internet dealers in the Nissan network, and we don't get that way by getting the figures wrong. In fact, we are one of the biggest Nissan dealers in Australia!
>
> We price match our cars daily to ensure we are very competitive, as we aren't located in a major city and we need to do this to entice customers through our door.
>
> I'm sure you know that car is very attractively priced, however there may be a goodwill gesture of a little bit of room to move. Realistically, what were you hoping to spend on... [list the car's age and spec]: £16,900 or £16,800? Something like that?

A caveat: if you're right in the middle of Sydney or London you might change the middle paragraph to:

> We price match our cars daily to ensure we are very competitive as we're located in the middle of London – with so much competition here we have to be very competitive all the time to attract customers through the door.

Let's talk about that last paragraph: am I negotiating with a customer who I don't really know? Not at all. When a customer asks for the best price and it's listed at £16,995 you can say, 'The best price is £16,995,' and we'll never hear from that customer again. Your second choice is to say, 'Well, it's up for £16,995, how much were you hoping to pay for it?' That's when the customer is going to come back and kick you where it hurts and say £15,000. Your third choice is, 'It's up for £16,999, but you know what, I'll do it for £16,800,' and now the customer's got *your* figure. And as soon as they've got your figure, they're going to continue shopping to satisfy their fundamental need for comparison.

What we do is condition the customer. We say: 'I might have a little bit of room to move. Realistically, what were you hoping to spend on a 2019 Honda Civic, £16,900 or £16,800, something like that?' We want the customer's *real* price, not the asking figure. They're likely to come back and say, 'I don't want to pay more than £16,500,' because they're thinking they're dealing with a salesperson who's willing to negotiate. So, let's stroke the greed gene and when the customer comes back with the new figure we can say:

> If we could agree to the figures on the.................. car we would require £1,000 to secure the car on a credit or debit card.
> We are not allowed to take that online - what is the best phone number to secure that car for you?

We're not negotiating, we're engaging. I want to engage with the customer to take them from the email inquiry to the telephone inquiry, and from the telephone inquiry I want to identify where they live to see if I can get them in for a visit.

Sometimes people are braver online – we call them keyboard warriors and the keyboard warrior might give you a silly figure. It's up for £16,995 and they might say: 'I'll give you £12,000.' Please don't respond with, *'If we could agree £12,000 we're going to require £1,000...'* because you'll raise the customer's expectation and when you come back at £16,900 you're going to drop them right down. If their offer is miles away, try:

> Thank you for your offer on the car, unfortunately that price is not going to be feasible for a... [spec of car]. How flexible could you be?

Is that car available?

What do you say other than yes? We can't go into a negotiation because the customer hasn't asked for our best price or for a discount. Every customer has the right to pay full price, and you know if it's the car they've been looking for you might be surprised when they simply say, 'That's the one I want.'

Try this:

> **Personalise and thank the customer for the enquiry!**
>
> The good news is that car you've enquired about has just come into stock* and is still available. I've just walked around the car and it's in great condition. I've taken the liberty of taking a video of the car for you. This will come in a separate email.
>
> All our used cars have been approved by BMW Select, part of BMW's high standard approved used car programme.
>
> If you would like an idea what your car is worth please give me a call or send me its registration number and I'll be happy to help.
>
> If you have any further questions please give me a call on 12345.

*Please don't tell a customer it's just come into stock when it hasn't.

In the modern world, we are lucky to be able to leverage so much technology to get this information to the customer. There are companies like 'CitNow' and '360 videos', or use 'iJot' on your iPhone to easily take a video of the car, talking about the things that are important in that car to the customer. If you want to see a sample video go to www.symcotraining.co.uk/bookresources and I'll show you some of the best ways to do a video.

Keep the video to about a minute and a half. Don't talk about the specifications of the car or do a features dump. If the customer has done sixteen hours and forty-two minutes of research they know all that stuff already. You need to introduce yourself, so include something along the lines of:

> 'Hi, my name's Simon. It's always nice to put a face to the name so you know who's working for you behind the computer.'

Then turn around and show them the car.

> 'As you can see the car's in great condition. I brought it in for a part exchange myself from a lovely couple who emigrated to Australia – that's why the mileage of the car is just 14,962km.'

Show the actual mileage!

> 'Now this car's in great condition, it's so rare to see a car that hasn't had at least one alloy wheel with a scuff for scrape on it. Even down to the tyres, a tyre has got 8mm on it when it's brand new, and in this case, it's still got 6mm of tread, so it's still got a good life on it. The only thing I've noticed about this car is there's a bit of a stone chip along the front there. We will get that touched up for you, but I thought you'd like to see it before you actually come see the car.'

Show them the car in the video. It's amazing how many times people watch that video, again and again and again. They are raising their desire before they ever get to see you.

If you're not doing videos yet, start doing them – now!

Wrapping it up... inject some urgency

There are some ways we can create urgency, the fourth fundamental, in an email. Try these:

> I know a lot of salespeople will tell you this, however you've seen that car on Autotrader and they give us a lot of information, like how many people viewed the car, how many times or page views, even the location of the people viewing the car. Just to let you know, out of all the Symco group stock, that was the third most viewed car this week. So, may I make a suggestion that we arrange an appointment sooner than later...

All of this goes out the window if the customer's local, because I believe the further away a customer is when they enquire about a used car, the hotter they are. If they are a local customer, a drive of anything up to an hour, you might go straight into:

> Getting the price right is the easiest part of my job because we are part of the Symco Group and we are one of the biggest internet retailers in the............ Network, however if the car is not exactly right for you, no price is going to be good enough.

> When is a good time to get together to ensure the car is exactly right for you? Would you prefer weekends or weekdays?

From here hopefully we get to speak to the customer and we've moved them through the process. When we talk to them, we can ask for an appointment, and then we need to confirm it.

Most businesses are very professional – but the motor trade sometimes gets left behind. Here's an example: my wife goes to a small beautician, that's run professionally. She gets a text reminder the day before an appointment, she has an app where she can collect points, and when she collects enough she gets a free treatment. It's a tiny place with just two or three people working there. We're selling a £30,000 or £60,000 car and sometimes we don't send an email confirmation! And we wonder why the customer doesn't turn up. Please send it.

Thank you for your time on the phone today. This email confirms our appointment for Sunday, January 12 at 11:00am. I will ensure the car you are looking at is ready for us to take a demonstration drive. Would you please bring your driver's licence for insurance purposes?

To get the best price on your car, when you bring your car, could you bring along the following:

- Service history, any invoices you may have for the car, and if you have any pre-paid service vouchers*

- MOT certificate

- Spare keys

- V5 registration document / log book

- Current finance settlement figure / GMFV

- Your paint and fabric protection certificate

Just ask for me when you come in – I will get the keys for the car and put them in my pocket so one of the other salespeople doesn't take it while we are waiting for you.

Would you like me to send you directions to the dealership?

I look forward to seeing you on Sunday, if something pops up and you can't make it would you please give me a call. If not I'll be especially waiting for you.

Simon

Do we need the customer's driver's license for insurance purposes? Maybe yes, maybe no, but I like to ask for it because I know I'm definitely going to need it to get the customer's finance approved. So, let's make sure they have everything with them.

When we ask them to bring in 'pre-paid service vouchers' we've increased the urgency again.

We don't need to spell out what the GMFV is, because we want the customer to ask, 'What's that?' and we've got engagement.

Notice we've said, 'Your paint and fabric protection certificate,' because when a customer asks what that is, you can say, 'That's a shame, the boss normally pays extra when we've got that paint and fabric protection certificate. It's this product called Super Guard...' and now you can send through the Super Guard video to the customer before they even turn up, sowing the seeds for those bolt-on accessories.

Of course, don't actually get the keys and pop them in your pocket, your boss will go mad, but it's a great way to make sure the customer asks for you by name when they turn up.

The final bit, 'Would you like me to send you directions to the dealership?' is a great qualifier. I used to go and get the dealership's directions and send them to the customer, but we found by accident this line works better because some people say, 'Yes thanks, I'm coming from miles away,' or 'I'm just around the corner and I pass you every day on the way to work.' Now we've got more information. Between the email and telephone, we should have customers half qualified.

SIX

Waypoint 2: Telephone

It's Good to Talk

Have you noticed that more customers are phoning in before they walk into the dealership? People do their research online before-hand, and when they call in they just want to get to the deal quickly. What we're going to look at now is how to take that initial inquiry into an appointment that actually turns up so you can get into the Road to a Sale process.

Let's compare the sales process for a walk-in customer to a telephone inquiry. With a walk-in customer we start with the attitude, we've got to get that right. Then we do the meet and greet: we use the part exchange as a qualifying tool, we go to the presentation, the demonstration, ask a nice trial close question to make sure we're on track, negotiate, and then we close. With the Road to a Sale walk-in process the close is actually on the car. Now compare that process with a telephone inquiry. First, you've got to get your attitude right, next you've got to meet and greet (you know, say hello!), then qualify and find out what they're looking for, find out their needs and wants, and then what? We want the appointment. On the telephone Road to a Sale process, the close is the appointment.

Walk-in Customer	Telephone Enquiry
attitude	attitude
meet & greet	meet & greet
qualify (use the part exchange)	qualify (needs & wants)
the presentation	~~the presentation~~
the demonstration	~~the demonstration~~
trial close	~~trial close~~
negotiate	~~negotiate~~
close (sell the car)	close (book the appointment)

You can see that on the telephone inquiry we miss some of the crucial steps – raising the desire.

Frequently on the telephone we try to raise the desire of the car – which is wrong! What we need to do is raise the desire on the appointment. In this section we're going to talk about why a customer needs to come and see *you* at your dealership. Let's be honest, if it's a new car they can get that new car from lots of different places – so we're going to talk about how to take that initial inquiry and go for the appointment.

Remember, there are only four reasons why a customer would come to see you as opposed to your competitors:

1. **Stock**
2. **Price**
3. **Location**
4. **You**

Let's have a look at how we can use them.

A question for you, who would you prefer to speak to: a walk-in or a telephone inquiry? Let me put it this way, if you got the chance to speak to a telephone inquiry but you missed the walk-in, or you speak to the walk-in and miss the telephone inquiry, which do you prefer? I'd probably agree with your first thought and go straight for the walk-in, but in reality, it's probably the telephone inquiry who is closer to a buying decision than the walk-in. You'll get a few time wasters and tyre-kickers walking in on a Saturday morning, but you'd have to be pretty sad to waste your time phoning up dealerships. Telephone enquirers are probably closer to a buying decision than the walk-ins, which is why I always prefer a telephone enquiry.

The first thing we need to look at is getting our attitude right on the telephone.

It's not what you say, it's the way that you say it

Experts tell us that 7% of what we communicate on a face-to-face basis is the words we use, and 38% is not what we say, but how we say it. My mother taught me that with a clip around the ear – it's not what you said, it's how you said it! And the remaining 55% is non-verbal communication or body language.

A study by Albert Mehrabian at UCLA University[1] showed that human communication around feelings and attitudes can be broken into three main parts:

---

1   http://www.iojt-dc2013.org/~/media/Microsites/Files/IOJT/11042013-Albert-Mehrabian-Communication-Studies.ashx

- 7% of the message is in the **words** that are spoken

- 38% of the message is the **way the words are said**

- 55% of the message is in the **facial expression** (or non-verbal communication)

This study is often misused as it was a study of how we communicate the emotions of love. However, it still makes sense in our setting. Words are just one part of your communication, it's how we say them that makes the difference.

A woman, without her man, is nothing.

Seems a bit sexist? It's not what you say – it's how you say it. Let's change the punctuation, change *how* you say it...

A woman: without her, man is nothing!

That's a 180-degree change in meaning, just by *how* we said the same words.

The other part of our communication is non-verbal or body language, and of course that's the bit that we miss on the phone.

Whenever you speak to someone on the telephone your mind generates images of the person you are dealing with. That image is generated by the way they communicate. Over the phone we lose all the non-verbal communication, so the other parts compensate for the lack of body language clues. Over the phone our communication can be broken down into two parts:

- 20% are the words

- 80% is how we use them

So, as you're reading through the telephone word tracks remember: it isn't just what you say, it's how you say it. The way you say the words is more important than the actual tracks. Take the tracks, twist them, and make them your own.

Before we get started with the tracks, go and find a Yellow Pages (if you can, I haven't seen one for years) and pick ten numbers at random. Give those companies a call and see if you can identify what they do from the way they answer your call. I bet you can't identify half of them. Why? Because they'll have got through their introduction and meet and greet before they've even taken a breath! Here are my steps for getting your phone attitude just right.

1. Before you pick up the telephone take a deep breath, or count to one, so you can get the phone to your head before you begin speaking. Sounds like common sense, however – as Nick Sewell once told me – common sense is not that common.

2. Talk a touch louder. No need to shout, but increase the volume a bit because it's impossible to mumble when you're talking louder. We tend to talk quietly when we're keeping secrets or trying to hide something, and the customer may think you're trying to hide something and not trust you. So, speak up.

3. Talk a touch slower. Not for the whole call, or the customer will think you're a bit thick. But, just for the opening, talk a touch slower.

4. Stand up or walk around. This opens the diaphragm and will alter the effect of your voice. It also gets more oxygen flowing to our brains.

5. Now take the caller through the process. Ask questions. Stop the customer asking you questions by taking them through the process.

Telephone script cheat sheet

This process comes from a man called Tom Stuker, an American sales trainer. Lots of other sales training companies train similar scripts, however, I think Tom's genius still works great... Usually when a customer calls in, they ask you a question and you answer. Then they ask you another question, and on it goes, with the customer leading the process. Once they have all the information they want, they'll go.

Over at our website we have a cheat sheet for you to download: www.symcotraining.co.uk/bookresources – print it out and keep it by the telephone for the next time someone calls in.

Using 'alternatives' questions to find out their needs and wants

What we need to do is trade information – we won't give them what they want until we get what we want. How? By taking their initial question and answering it with a question. Throughout the whole process we'll be answering their questions with our 'alternatives' questions.

Here are some alternatives-type questions: red wine or white wine? Apple juice or orange juice? Beer or spirits? Tea or coffee? Still or sparkling water? Do you find your mind automatically and easily answering these types of questions? Alternatives questions are great because they give us control and they're easy for the customer to answer. Here are some car alternatives questions:

'Can you give me the price on the Civic?'

'Of course, can I ask you, was that a new or used Civic?'

'New.'

'Oh, a new one. Do you prefer petrol or Hybrid?'

> **Do you prefer the poverty pack or the bling-bling model? Manual or automatic? The three-door or five-door?**

These alternatives questions are powerful, and each one can branch off until we get to know what the customer actually wants. These types of questions open up the customer and get us into a more conversational tone.

With new car customers you can add in car colour preferences: do you prefer lighter or darker colours? Don't ask for a specific colour preference, as they may pick a colour that you can't get any stock of, like Iridescent Snowflake. Just ask for light or dark. Their answer will tell you if they've been shopping around a lot, because if they ask for a specific colour (like Iridescent Snowflake!) they've likely been shopping and this can help you.

A great track if a customer asks for a specific car is:

> **'There are three or four different models of that car – which one have you been researching online?'**

Now I know not everyone's been researching online, but most people have and when they tell you they want the S-Line model, you can follow up with: 'Great, what was it about the S-Line model that put it on your shopping list?' Find out what *selling* the customer's done to themselves already.

Getting information from the customer

So, we've used our alternatives questions to qualify what the customer is looking for. Now we need to get some information from the customer – and we do this by implying we're going to call them back.

> 'Great, Mr Customer, what I'm going to do is have a quick check to see what we've got in stock at the moment, but while I'm doing that let me check with the manufacturer to see if we've got any price advantage cars coming through. Now that should take me ten to fifteen minutes or so. Tell me, where are you calling from, home or work?'

Look at that – we're back to an alternatives question again. The human mind can't not answer the question. They're going to answer, and you can just follow up with:

> 'And your number there is?'

They'll tend to spit it out without even thinking. Now you can go into:

> 'And your name is?'

We find 90% of the time we get the customer's name and number. So, now you have their name, their number, and the car they're interested in – and the customer thinks you're going to be calling them back. You might be thinking you're going to call them right back – but stop! If you do call them back the customer's phone is likely to be busy, because they're already calling the next dealership from the 'locate your nearest dealership' list they found on the internet.

I was taught to say to a customer, 'I'm away from my desk right now,' or 'I'm just talking to another customer right now, what's your name and number and I'll give you a call right back.' Don't do that – it's old fashioned and worse, it tells the customer that you're not that interested in them as they're not as important as the other customer. So, even though I've implied I'm going to call them back, this is where I stop and say:

> 'In fact, I might be able to save you a bit of time. Is it okay if I have a real quick check for you while you're on the phone?'

They're always going to say yes because they want the information. Then, get off the phone for about fifteen seconds and check your stock list.

Remember, we also used the words 'price advantage' – what did that mean? Well, everything and nothing! It's a phrase none of your competitors use. If the customer phones up one Honda dealership they might just get the retail price. They phone another and get a fully discount price. Then they phone you and you tell them that you sometimes get special price advantage cars. Do you think they might be interested? Maybe a little bit curious? Do you think they will want to come and speak to you? You bet! Now, I live in the real world and know it's not going to work all the time – but you have definitely got their attention. That's what we're doing here – stop the shopping.

How much do we need to discount a car to make it price advantaged? A full £1,000 or even just fifty pence! Price advantaged means everything and nothing.

Back to our customer with an alternatives question – not 'if' they can come and see us, but 'when':

> 'Are you there, Mr Jones? The good news is I've got two or three cars that should suit what you're looking for. When's a good time for you to pop in to have a look at these? This afternoon, or maybe tomorrow morning?'

You'll be surprised how many customers agree to an appointment because you've gone back to the alternatives questions. Other great alternatives for an appointment: Saturday or Sunday? Earlier or later?

Used car variations

In the past, customers would call in asking if a specific model was in stock, and you'd have a look for them. It doesn't happen that way very often anymore. Occasionally, someone will be looking for rare stock and calling around, but in my experience most customers are inquiring about a specific used car. So, let's look at the four fundamentals.

How can we use scarcity?

Let's imagine a customer calls about that one specific used car, 'Is that car still available? And if so, what's the best price?'

The poor salesperson will go ahead, answering the customer's questions, letting the customer direct the conversation. Once the customer has everything they need, they're gone.

When a customer asks about a specific used car you need to first qualify which car. Ask some questions: 'Do you have the registration number? Where did you see it? Was it on our forecourt or was it online? What website was that, our website or the manufacturer's website?' Then:

> 'I was on a day off yesterday. I can normally see that car parked at the front of the dealership just from my desk, but I notice it's been moved. I've got a funny feeling we might have taken a deposit on it. If that car has sold what else did you see on our website that caught your attention?'

I promise you every time the customer will say, 'No, no, it's just that one!' Now I'm not advocating lying about being on a day off if you weren't. However, in the real world, cars are moved all the time. Let's gently take the car away from the customer. Remember people often want what they can't have.

> 'Ok, while I check and see if that's available, I'll also check to see what other used cars we've got coming into stock that are not on the website yet. That should take me ten to fifteen minutes or so. Where are you calling from, home or work?'

Can we add a bit of urgency?

Once you have the registration number and you know the customer has seen the car on auto trader or another website you might say:

> 'I know a lot of salespeople will tell you this, but you've seen that car on Autotrader and they give us a lot of information, like how many people viewed the car, how many times or page views, even down to the location of the people viewing the car.
>
> Just to let you know, out of all the Symco group stock that was the second most viewed car this weekend and I'm just one of seventy salespeople in our group who can sell it. So, I just need to check to see if it's available. If that car has sold what else did you see on our website that caught your attention?'

Here's another response. I stole this idea from a man called Pete Smith; it's a bit cheeky. I've used it myself and it works brilliantly. It might be too far for you, but I'll let you decide. Whenever Pete gets the registration number of the car the customer's looking for he says: 'Great, let me go and have a quick check to see if that's available on the system.' He lets the customer hear him tap away on the computer, then he says, 'Ah right, it was Dave you were speaking to this morning. Is that Mr Casey?' The customer will always say no, that he didn't call in. Pete replies, 'I'm sorry, it must be someone else. Listen I just need to check with my colleague to see if that car's still available.' This is brilliant because Pete is using the laws of scarcity *and* urgency, you might want to try that for the specific used car customer.

A little word of warning: I have had salespeople hear this technique and turn it into 'lots of people have phoned about that car so you better be quick'. This approach often leads to: 'If it sells, it sells', or 'If it's meant to be, it's meant to be'. Put yourself in the customer's shoes. If lots of people have called about the car and it hasn't sold, there must be something wrong with it.

So that's the basic format that Tom Stuker came up with years ago. You need to make it sound like you, you need to feel comfortable with the words. Download the cheat sheet we looked at earlier (you'll find it on our website) and keep it by your phone.

Handling Objections

In the real world you're going to get some objections. Let's take a look at how you can handle them.

OBJECTION 1: What is your best price?

People go straight in and ask what your best price is. You've got six ways to deal with that process.

Number 1:

> 'Getting the price right is the easiest part of my job, however if the car is not exactly right for you, no price is going to be good enough. When is a good time for you to pop in to make sure the car is exactly right for you? Weekends or week days?'

I like to start with this technique because the customer has two choices: either they say, 'Yeah, you're right Simon, I do need to make sure the car's right. I'll pop in this weekend,' or 'No, I know the car is right for me, just tell me the price.' Right at the beginning of the call you've got the customer telling you that car is perfect for them!

So, what do we say if they know it's the right car for them, and they just want the best price?

Number 2:

> 'The best price will be the lowest amount of money coming out of your pocket. We need to have a look at the car you're trading in so we can get the best balance to change and monthly payments. When would be a good time for us to have a look at your car, weekends or week days?'

What if they resist – they don't want to waste their time and ask for a ballpark figure on their car over the phone?

Number 3:

> 'You see the trouble with giving any price over the phone is it's going to end up being a guess, and I'm going to end up guessing too high or I'm going to end up guessing too low.
>
> If I guess too high, you're just going to be upset with me when I can't give you that figure when I see your car. In fact, some dealers out there will give you a price over the phone that they know they can't do just to get you to come in. I'm not going to play those games with you.
>
> If I guess too low, we're never going to see each other. What I prefer to do is not guess at all, but show you exactly what we can do when we see the car.
>
> So, when is a good time for us to have a look at your car? Weekends or week days?'

What if they still insist they don't want to waste their time and money unless the figures are right?

Number 4:

> 'Getting the money right, as I said, is the easiest part of my job and I'm so confident we'll get the money right that if I can't, I am more than willing to pay for your fuel to get you back home. I can't be fairer than that, can I? So, when is a good time for us to get together? Weekends or week days?'

You might be thinking I'm mad – this could cost you a fortune in fuel! Only use this on a new car customer. And remember, for a customer to claim the money on fuel, number one they have to turn up, and number two if the price you've done is not as good as somewhere else, naturally as a great salesperson you'll say: 'That surprised me, getting the money right is normally the easy part of my job. Realistically, what sort of balance is that other dealer talking about…?' and you'll match the deal.

Don't use this technique on used cars because you might be comparing prices with an independent dealer with lower overheads than you. You might want to check with your sales manager first.

Number 5:

If a customer is calling from a long distance, more than an hour and a half away, first still ask for the appointment, you might be shocked that they come to your town regularly anyway. If they say it's too far away, try this:

> 'Normally Mr Customer, when someone phones me from that far away about a new car they're just trying to keep their local deal honest. I can't blame you, I'd be doing the same thing. Is that what you're trying to achieve?'

They might admit to it, or they might say they'd never buy from their local dealer. If they'd never buy from that dealer then you know something went wrong and you're on the way to selling a car. If they admit to just trying to keep their local dealer honest:

> 'I can't blame you, I'd be doing the same thing. Tell me what deal you've got and I'll tell you if you got a great deal.'

Every time they tell you the deal say,

> 'Wow that is a brilliant deal. How much better than that deal would we have to be to get you to drive two hours?'

It won't work all the time – but it's definitely worth a try.

Number 6:

If someone is really pushing me, I *will* sell a car over the phone. I'll go for the appointment every single time first, but if you don't sell them a car someone else will. Having said that, it's important to go for the trial close first, and look for the commitment:

'Let me share this with you. We all buy cars from exactly the same place –Toyota Australia. We all buy them at exactly the same price and we all have exactly the same restrictions*. What I mean by that is that any price we could do, one of our competitors could do as well. But it would be silly of me to give my commercial advantage out over the phone.

For all I know you might be another Toyota dealer wondering how we're selling so many of these Yaris'. You don't sound like one, but the price I can do – if you give it to one of my competitors, you'd get me into a bit of trouble.

So, let me ask you, if I can get the figures right, are you in a position to leave me £1,000 on a credit or debit card?'

*Don't use the word margins, because customers think you have huge margins!

Try these six different steps to overcome the objection of 'What's your best price?' Always aim for the appointment first because it's so much easier to sell the car when we get them face-to-face and we can raise the customer's desire through the sales process.

Confirming The Appointment

We've done all the hard work and they're coming in for the appointment – but now we need to make sure they ask for *you*. Let's look at setting up a firm appointment.

'Right Mr or Mrs Customer, do you have a pen ready? My name is Simon Bowkett, that's B O W K E T T. When you pop in, if you just ask for Simon or the Aussie, that tends to find me. That's 11 o'clock on Saturday morning. Now if something pops up and you can't make it, would you please give me a call? Otherwise I'll be especially waiting for you.'

You could try a trick that I heard from Colin McAllister, ask the customer to pause again: 'Could you hold the phone for a second, I just need to get the appointment book.' Get off the phone for five or ten seconds and then get back on the call: 'Are you there Mr Customer? Good news is 11 o'clock on Sunday morning is fine. But someone else is driving that car at 12 o'clock, is that hour going to give you enough time or do you want to make it a touch earlier?' You'd be amazed how many times you try that and the customer asks to come earlier or even right now.

This trick from Colin is telling customers that the car is scarce and injecting a bit of urgency. He's going back to the four fundamentals.

Once the person's got the pen and they've written down the time, we need to make sure we've got their postal address and the email address, so say:

'Let me send you through some information – what's your postcode so I can send that through to you?... And the house number? In fact, Mr Customer, in the modern world it's probably easier if I email you, let me email you some information now. What's the best email address to send that to? Is that a work or private one? And that address is...'

See what I'm doing there with 'That address is...' – that's a probe. A probe is a question where you say half the statement, ending with an open pause and the customer just finishes it.

How many customers are turning up without their trade-ins or part exchanges? That's just more work! Let's try to nip that in the bud.

> **'I'll send that information right now. By the way, the car that you're looking to trade in, what is it? And the mileage on that? Wow, that's something we'd definitely be interested in. Listen, when you bring your car can you also bring the logbook, the service history, and any invoices you might have for repairs or improvements to get the best money for your car? I look forward to seeing you at 11 o'clock on Sunday morning.'**

Now you can send the email confirmation that we talked about in the last chapter.

When confirming the appointment, we should try and change the time. If the appointment is for 11 o'clock on Sunday morning try saying: 'Oh, hold on for a second, Mr Customer, is there a chance I could make that quarter to eleven or quarter past?' Doctors do that. Airlines do that. They don't give you a doctor's appointment at 11 o'clock. People are more likely to turn up when it's a specific time. It tells the customer you're busy, you work to a schedule and it will help ensure they turn up at the appointed time.

For telephone call scripts for following up with a customer, take a look at Waypoint 4.

SEVEN

Waypoint 3: The Visit

The Bum Is on the Seat

The bum is (almost) on the seat – now you need to raise the desire and bring into play your four fundamentals.

Meet and greet

When a customer comes into your business, you need to start building rapport. Remember, lots of your customers are going to be apprehensive, nervous, or even scared when they come into your business. They love the idea of buying a new car but aren't entirely sure about the buying process.

With this in mind, here are a few of the actual meet and greet phrases I have heard with my own ears in car dealerships around the world.

- 'Has someone got to you yet?' Has someone got to me yet? That's what I'm worried about.

- 'Are you right bud?' Are they talking about my right bud? Is that some sort of euphemism?

- 'What's the story?' To be fair, that one was in Ireland and seemed to work well if I recall.

I had a salesperson who one day said to a customer, 'I know you from somewhere, are you off the telly or something?'

The customer replied, 'We bought a car from you yesterday, we just need to drop our insurance certificate off...'

What about the one meet and greet phrase that I hear the most?

'Can I help you?'

I would urge you to avoid this opening phrase, because whatever retail environment you work in, most of the time the response will be: 'No thanks, I'm just looking.' This is a closed question and the response can only be yes, no, or I'm just looking. This is a *predictable response*.

Don't believe me? Think of a flower...

A large percentage of the population will think of a rose. If I ask you to think of the colour of that rose, an even larger percentage of the population will think of a red rose. We've been conditioned to think of this combination over the years with so many Valentine's Day adverts. These are predictable responses. Not everyone will think of that combination. The colour that jumps into my head is actually yellow – as that is my wife's favourite colour of rose. However, a large enough percentage of population think red to make it a predictable response.

The predictable response of a customer to the phrase, 'Can I help you?' is 'No, I'm just looking.' In fact, some customers may even say, 'I'm just looking,' out of habit. Have you ever walked into a shop and initially told the assistant that you were just looking and then when you had a question about their product, you spent the next half an hour looking for someone to help you?

These are great examples of the poor salesperson's way of meeting and greeting. How *should* you do it? Let's have a look at some better word tracks, but first let me introduce you to the Gap!

Mind the Gap

I want to introduce a concept called Gap selling. Not Guaranteed Asset Protection, I'm talking about finding out the gap from the customer's current situation to the desired situation.

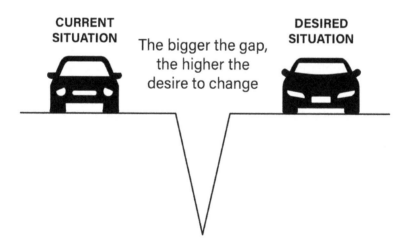

CURRENT SITUATION The bigger the gap, the higher the desire to change **DESIRED SITUATION**

Figure 5.1 The mind gap

In this image you can see the customer's current situation on the left, and the desired situation on the right, and in between there is a gap. In other words, a gap is just a reason to buy – and if there wasn't a gap, they wouldn't be looking to buy.

This gap can be lots of different sizes. Let's imagine that as I put my suit on this morning, the hem fell down. If I had bought this suit only six weeks ago, would I go and buy a brand new suit? Probably not, because the gap would be too small for me to want to buy something new again. However, if as I put my suit on this morning I put my leg right through the crotch, tripped and tipped a hot cup of coffee over myself, and standing on one leg hopping around like a nutter I managed to spill a glass of wine from the night before down the other leg – would I now go and buy a brand-new suit? I probably would, because the gap would be a lot bigger.

The bigger the gap, the higher the desire there is to change. The higher the desire, the more urgency there is to change. The four fundamentals come into play: urgency and desire, or in other words, value in the product. We're looking for some sort of problem the customer has, because once we've found a problem, we can provide a solution.

How do we find out what problems the customer has? We ask questions about their part exchange or trade-in. Simple questions to find out what they like most, what they don't like, and why they're looking to change. Once we have these answers, we can show how the new vehicle will provide solutions to their problems.

That problem can be real or perceived. A real problem could be they've got a three-door sports car, they're about to have a baby, and they need more space before the child arrives. A perceived problem might be that the in-laws are coming over from Australia and they want the new car before they turn up. Or they've moved house and they want to impress their new neighbours. Or their brother-in-law has a car with 2018 plates and they want one with 2019 plates.

Our job is to ask questions to discover the problem and offer a solution. Simple.

I was taught to sell the customer with: feature, advantage, benefit. I'm so old now that when I first started training most cars didn't have power steering as standard, so this is what I would say: 'Mr or Mrs Customer, is there something you haven't got in your car that you'd like in the new car?' When they reply that they want power steering: 'This vehicle has got power steering, which means that it keeps it nice and light – so the next time you're in a tight parking situation you don't need strong-arm steering. That would be good, wouldn't it?'

Feature: This vehicle has got power steering

Advantage: Nice and light

Benefit: Easier to park

Let me ask you a question: whose reasons are more important, the salesperson's or the customer's? It's got to be the customer's.

We still use feature-advantage-benefit selling and I'm not saying it's wrong, but if people have done sixteen hours and forty-two minutes of research online before they email, phone, or walk into your dealership do you think they know the advantages of the power steering before they got to you? Of course! So you need to use gap selling. Quite simply, find that gap and then gently take it away from them; people want what they can have. By gently taking it away they'll start selling the advantages of it to themselves.

Say you have a customer asking for a used vehicle that you haven't got in stock – for example, a used diesel. If you ask, 'does it have to be a diesel?' the customer will give you a hundred reasons why they must have a diesel: 'It's got to be a diesel because I do 4,000 miles a year, that's a lot of mileage you know. And the price of fuel is going up.' Now we're in a funny place called stuck – even though we know 4,000 miles is not a lot of miles. They've sold the diesel to themselves, and you don't have a car to satisfy the need.

Which one of these has more saleability, the old feature-advantage-benefit way as taught by lots of sales trainers, or this one?

> **'Mr Customer, is there something you haven't got in your car that you'd really like in the new car?'**
>
> 'Power steering.'
>
> **'OK, we've got power steering across the whole range now, but why is that important to you? Is that something you must have?'**
>
> 'Yes. I've got to have power steering because my wife's got arthritis and it makes it really difficult for her to get into a tight parking spot – and our driveway is quite tight.'

Now, we can take that information, and when we present a car instead of using feature-advantage-benefit we can say: 'The power steering on this car is going to make your wife's life a lot easier, isn't it?'

We can also use that information for negotiating. When the customer baulks at the monthly payments: 'Mr Customer, I know it's £20 a month more than you wanted to pay, however it does have the power steering and that will make your wife's life a lot easier.' We are hinting that he thinks his wife is not worth £20 a month – now I would never say that, but I will imply it.

Let's have a look at that same concept for the modern world. How many people want leather interior, adaptive cruise control, the smart city brake support, active lane departure warning systems, etc? If someone has asked for an active lane departure warning system early on the process, they've probably done some selling to themselves long before they got to you.

So, how do we use the gentle take away?

> **'Yes, we've got active lane departure warning system on the bling-bling model, but why is that so important to you? Is that something you must have?'**
>
> 'I've got to have the active lane departure warning system because when I hired a car in Florida recently I was looking at the satellite navigation trying to find my way to Orlando, and if it wasn't for that system I wouldn't be here today, because we started veering into another lane and the active lane departure warning system put us back in the centre. I wouldn't want a car without that now.'

Now, when we start selling the car with the active lane departure warning system, they've almost sold it to themselves.

OBJECTION 1: 'I'm Just Looking...'

'How can I help you?' might seem like an OK option as it's an open question, however you will find that you will still get lots of people who will respond with, 'I'm just looking.'

What about this one: 'Hi, welcome to Symco Mercedes. My name is Simon, how can I help you today?' followed by an outstretched hand.

It sounds professional, but if the customer is a bit apprehensive to start with, we might scare them off if we go straight out to them and lean forwards with a handshake. If you walk straight up to a customer you're invading their personal space. Remember those comfort zones we talked about earlier? If someone encroaches into that personal space, our adrenaline starts building to enable us to fight or flight, like back in the caveman days. You don't want to be a 'space invader'.

1. 'What brings you here today?'

It's probably better to start with some small talk, maybe something as simple as: 'Hi, how are you? What brings you here today?'

'What brings you here today?' is a good question, not least because it's harder to answer with, 'I'm just looking'. More often than not, though, I've found that customers will mention a particular product or a problem they face. It's the same in every industry: 'We were thinking of moving to the area, our family's growing and we need a three-bedroom house, not two,' for example.

So, if a customer tells you they want to look at a particular product, this is your cue to ask them: 'OK, great, what was it about the Audi Q5 that put it on your shopping list?'

Then it's imperative to shut up and listen – just like Parky. Find out what sort of a selling job the customer has already done to him or herself.

And of course, there's: 'Have you found what you're looking for?'

Initially I didn't like this one because it goes against the grain. We're trained to ask open-ended questions when we meet and greet. I was in a car dealership and I stole this idea from a colleague named Mike Thompson. It's actually a closed question. But when you think about it, it works really well.

Mike goes out and asks the customer: 'Have you found what you're looking for?'

The only answers you could get from a customer are: 'Yes,' 'No,' or, 'I'm just looking.'

If they say yes, you ask them, 'Which one caught your eye? Oh, the Audi Q5. Great, what was it about the Audi Q5 that put it on your shopping list?'

If the customer says no you can respond with, 'OK, what were you looking for? The new Land Rover Discovery? OK, we've got those over here. What was it about the Land Rover Discovery that put it on your shopping list?'

Try this approach and see how it works for you. But do bear in mind – this isn't an open invitation to use closed questions at the meet and greet. Don't start asking 'Can I help you?' because you know the answer will be, 'No thanks, I'm just looking.'

2. 'Other than just having a good look around…' or 'Other than just looking…'

Here's one from the other end of the spectrum. A lot of the time, you can tell if a customer is going to say, 'I'm just looking' before you even go to meet and greet them. They avoid making eye contact, they seem apprehensive, and may have their hands deep in their pockets – metaphorically protecting their money. You can often nip the, 'I'm just looking' response in the bud with something along the lines of: 'Other than just having a good look around, what particular car/watch/computer/etc. could I get you some information on?'

Saying 'other than just looking' can often stop that excuse from arising in the first place.

Don't default to this option though. Don't go straight into it as your only meet and greet technique. Save it for the boundary riders – the ones who stay as far away as possible and who you can almost hear whispering, 'Here he comes, here comes a salesperson,' to each other as you approach them.

3. The Columbo '... but tell me...'

Try using what is often called the Columbo Technique, after the TV detective. He asks his suspect all the important questions about a crime he's investigating. Things like what time they got to the party, when did they leave, did they arrive by themselves, did they leave by themselves, can they think of anything else that would help the investigation, and if they do later, here's my card – give me a call. But then, as he walks away, he would turn around and say: 'Just one more question. How long have you been sleeping with the maid?' He would catch the suspect off guard and thus solve the crime.

That's what we can do to our customer – get them to open up when they drop their guard. Despite your best efforts, they've said, 'No thanks, I'm just looking,' and have maybe even put their arms up in front of them as well, as a defensive gesture. Do the same. Put your hands up and step back. Putting your hands up goes back to the Stone Age. It signifies that you have no weapon and don't pose a threat. Open palms are good as well. 'No problem, sir. Make yourself at home and have a good look around.' Start to turn away and then say: 'But tell me, what sort of car/computer/TV/etc are you looking for? I might be able to point you in the right direction.'

At this point, some people will have lowered their barriers a bit and are more likely to tell you what it is they are looking for. 'OK, great, we've got one of those over here. Tell me, what was it about the Sony that put it on your shopping list?'

4. Signposting – hands up, then the Columbo

If that's not for you, try 'signposting' instead. It's called signposting because you are acting like a sign. It starts off like the last technique:

'No problem, make yourself at home and have a good look around.'

But then you add: 'Just to let you know, our used cars here are just a small selection of the cars that we have in our group stock. If we haven't got what you're looking for here, just ask – because there might one in our central compound. If it is a new car you're looking for, we can't fit everything in the showroom, so if we haven't got what you're looking for here just ask, as it might be out the back. We've got the brochures for everything over here, tea and coffee over there, and the toilets are just around the corner. Make yourself at home and have a good look around.'

Then just as you start to walk away, and hopefully the customer starts to drop their guard, add: 'But tell me, what sort of car were you looking for? I might be able to point you in the right direction.'

It will work in any retail environment: 'Just to let you know, the watches we've got here are just a small selection of what we have in stock. If we haven't got what you are looking for here, just ask because we might have one in the back… But tell me, what sort of watch were you looking for? I might be able to point you in the right direction.'

By telling people briefly where everything is in your store, you are setting the agenda and making the customer feel at ease.

5. Research day – 'Sometime in the future…'

So, the customer has said: 'No thanks, I'm just looking.'

You could respond with, 'Sure no problem. Let's call this your research day or information day. That way it takes a bit of pressure off both of us. I could give you all the information you need, so at some time in the future you will have everything you need to decide. What car can I get you some information on?'

At this point you might be thinking you don't really want to give your customer all the information they are asking for, so they can go away and think about it or shop your deal with a competitor. You're only going to lose them. I know that as well. But let's take the pressure off them – by not obligating them just yet.

Isn't that what happens with relationships too? 'Let's go out for a meal and see what happens, we might not even get along.' Of course, you want to get along or you wouldn't be going on a date! But you're not going to say that to start with. You would be in danger of scaring the other person off.

This technique is just about taking the pressure off and 'sometime in the future' can, of course, be five minutes from now. It gives us the opportunity to relax the customer so we can raise their desire – and you will be amazed how many times the same customer ends up saying 'I can't believe I've bought a boat today, I was just looking!'

6. 'Most of my customers…'

Here's another technique that's very similar to number five but with a slight twist. When a customer says 'I'm just looking,' you respond with:

'It would be my luckiest day if on the first visit you wanted to buy. If you're like most of my customers on their first visit, they just want to have a look at the new car and see if it's right for them.

They want to get an idea of what their car's worth, find out how much a month it's going to cost them, just so they've got all the information so sometime in the future they've got everything they need to make the right decision. Are you like most of my customers? Is that what you want to achieve today?'

This is designed to take the pressure off the customer.

OBJECTION 2: What's Your Best Price?

There are some other common objections you are going to get at the meet and greet stage. 'What's your best price?' is probably the next most common objection.

You will get customers who have already been on the internet, know what they want, and go straight into talking about price. In fact, don't most customers do their research on line before they get to us? In which case, we need to get back to selling ourselves and the product before we sell the deal. If we just talk about the deal before we raise the desire, we are going to risk losing it or at best securing a deal without maximizing the profit in it.

So, when a customer says right at the start: 'What's your best price on that? For cash, right now, what can you do?' try some of these word tracks.

1. 'No price is good enough...'

This is a simple and effective response:

> 'Sir, if we ever lose anyone's business it's never because of the price. Getting that right is the easiest part of my job. But unless the product is exactly right, no price is going to be good enough. So, let me just grab the keys and let's make sure it's the right car for you.'

It's a three-stage technique, let's look at each stage:

Stage 1: 'If we ever lose anyone's business it's never because of the price.' This tells people you are always competitive. People want to know they're not going to be wasting their time looking at your product if they're not going to be dealing with a company that can deliver the lowest price.

Stage 2: 'Getting the figures right is the easiest part of my job.' OK, in reality it might not be the easiest part of your job. It isn't always the easiest part of mine. But we need to relax the customer at this stage to allow us to build more value into the product or service, because when we have built more value it will be a much easier part of your job.

Stage 3: 'However, unless the product is exactly right, no price is going to be good enough.' A lot of salespeople struggle with this objection at this point in the sales process, because they don't know how to open the sale up. They start asking questions like, 'What price were you hoping to get it for?' or 'When are you looking to buy?' which can only lead to conflict as the customer is likely to say they wanted the product for a ridiculously low price or dig their heels in and throw the salesperson into a vicious circle of words with a, 'Well I don't know when I want to buy it, it all depends on your best price!' So try the simple three-stage technique above instead.

2. 'No, no, what's your best price?'

You might want try this:

> 'The best price will be the amount of money coming out of your pocket, so we need to get the details about the car you're going to trade in to get you the best balance to change, and monthly payments. What car are you looking to trade in?'

Notice how we didn't say to the customer, 'Do you have a car to part exchange or trade-in?' because many people say they haven't got a car to part exchange, so you negotiate the best deal on the new car and then they tell you they've changed their mind and throw in the part exchange.

3. 'Thank goodness...' slow down by speeding up (good for Lions)

Will the above technique work with every customer? Of course not. Some of your customers will say: 'You're not listening to me! I know what I want. I've done all of my research online. All I want to know is what your best price is!'

Always start with the three-stage process:

> 'Mr Customer, if we ever lose anyone's business, it's never because of the price. Getting that right is the easiest part of my job. But unless that product is exactly right for you, no price is going to be good enough. So, let's just make sure we've got exactly the right kitchen for you.'
>
> 'No, I know what I want, all I want to know is what you can do it at.'
>
> 'Thank goodness for that. Someone who actually wants to buy! I just spent three hours with my last customers and they aren't looking to change until next year. If you'd like to come in we can get that sorted for you.'

At this point your aggressive customer might take a step back: 'Er, I just want a price at this stage.' Sometimes they don't say anything, there is just a look of panic.

Then you can take the pressure off the customer by saying:

> 'I'm sorry, I'm rushing you. You haven't even had a chance to see if this product is right for you. I didn't even introduce myself either. I'm Simon. And you are? So, Mr Smith, what was it about this product that put it on your shopping list?'

And you are right back into your sales process. You are actually slowing the customer down by speeding them up.

OBJECTION 3: *'I Just Want a Brochure.'*

Another common objection at the meet and greet stage is where the customer says: 'Can I just have a brochure on such and such?' or 'Can I get some information on such and such?'

Now, if you give them your brochure, or other information, they are probably going to leave as soon as they've got it. Consequently, I was always taught to say: 'Oh, sorry, we haven't got a brochure on that at the moment. What's your name and address so I can get one sent out to you?'

The trouble with that, though, is that it sounds a bit unprofessional. The customer might be thinking, 'If they haven't even got a brochure, what else don't they have? Would they even have replacement parts?'

So, if you want to use this technique, make sure you 'accidentally' find a brochure to give to them after you've captured their contact details. Because in the 'now' world that we live in, they aren't going to wait for one to arrive in the post when they could have just as easily ordered one online. They are much more likely to go to your competitor and get one from there. So, make sure you give them a brochure!

There's an even better response, one that won't leave your potential customer thinking you're incompetent, disorganised, or worse, a liar!

The brochure as a qualifying tool...

I call this the Tony Sexton, because that's who I learned it from. He gets the brochure but keeps it in his hand to stop the customer leaving immediately. And he uses the specification sheet as a qualifying tool.

> 'Can I get a brochure on such and such?'
>
> **'Sure, no problem, I'll just go and get you one.'**

When he comes back with it, he says: 'OK, here's the brochure. Just let me show you how it works. We've got all the product info in the front here, the colours at the back, and the specifications are right in the middle. Now it actually comes in three different models. What are you driving at the moment? What are you comparing it with? Oh, a such and such. Well, you are probably looking at this model then. In fact, I've got the actual car over here, let me show you.'

Then, still holding the brochure, he turns around and walks over to the car. More often than not, he finds that the customer followed him. Try it and see if it works for you.

Part Exchange/Trade-In

'What's my car worth?' – I estimate that 80% of customers ask me this question within the first five minutes. When a customer visits the showroom, they have an agenda.

The Customer's Agenda:

1. Look at the car

2. Get a price on the new car

3. Get an idea of what their car is worth

4. Find out the balance to change or what the monthly payments will be

5. Then take it all home and think about it… which of course is code for let me shop around as much as I can

If people have done sixteen hours and forty-two minutes of research can they get information about a new car without speaking to a salesperson? Of course they can. Sometimes, they know more about the car than we do. Can they get the price on that new or used car without speaking to us? Of course they can. What they can't get without speaking to us is how much our dealership will offer them on their car, which is why 80% of people ask that question straight away.

The poor salesperson responds to that question with: 'Hold on for a second, I don't even know what car you're interested in.' The customer knows what they want, so that question doesn't work. I suggest we work with the grain and not against the grain. Let's set the agenda, something like this:

> 'Great, I'm happy to get that for you, let me show you the science we're going to use to come up the best price. We're not just going to look on a website or some guide or pluck it out of the air because I'm sure you've been to some web sites already.
>
> If you tell me all the good things about your car, I'll come and take some photos of it and then I'm going to go and give it to my boss. Even though it's a car we might sell ourselves here, what my boss will do is ring around some independent buyers to get the best money for your car. Effectively we'll do the shopping around for you. That's why we're one of the biggest dealers in the area.
>
> That's going to take twenty minutes or so, are you alright for time?'

That's called setting the agenda, we're telling them how we're going to come up with the best price. If I say their trade-in is worth 4,000 Euros and they don't like 4,000 Euros, they don't like me as a salesperson. If I say my boss or my sales manager says the car's worth 4,000 Euros, they don't like my boss. Would you deal with a company where you didn't like the boss? Maybe not. But by saying 'my boss has done some research, he's phoned around a few independent buyers and the market value is 4,000 Euros,' the customer can be upset with the market, not an individual. Later, when the customer invariably gets upset about the price, we can say,

> 'We work within a market, we don't create the market. The market value on your car is 4,000 Euros.'

Qualifying the customer

All too often I hear salespeople qualifying the deal, but not the customer. They use phrases like, 'A three-door or a five-door? A petrol or a diesel? A manual or automatic?' All good stuff – but don't forget there's three sales you need to make, and we need to sell yourselves first. Here are some word tracks that helped me:

> 'I see you're here on a Tuesday, are you on a day off or on holiday? What do you do for a living to get a day off in the middle of the week? You're a salesperson, what industry? Real estate agent, how's business at the moment?'

This is one way we could get to know the customer. A great way to qualify the customer is the part exchange. If you walked around my house would you learn a lot about me?

You would, you'd know almost right away as you walked into my home office that I'm the stereotypical foreigner. I've got a picture of a kangaroo hopping down the beach on my office wall. Don't judge me! If you walked around my house *with me* and saw the picture you could ask me questions about it, and you'd learn even more about me. That's why I suggest you take the customer with you when you go and look at their trade-in.

Too frequently I see salespeople looking at the customer's trade-in by themselves – and they've missed a great qualifying opportunity. Imagine you're with the customer and you see a tow bar on the back of their car, you can ask: 'What do you tow with that? Ah, a horse box? Are you into horses, Debs?' If you see a United sticker on the back of the car do you think that club is important to him? Of course it is; ask about it. Child seats in the back seat: 'Do you have a boy or girl? What age?'

This is how you qualify the *customer* and not just the deal. So always take the customer with you to look at their car. Build rapport, and let them build rapport with you.

Four ways to increase urgency

During the look around the car we have four opportunities to build urgency.

1. 'Is the next service a major one?'

> 'The next service is the 20,000 miles one, is that the major service on this car?'

What have we put in our customer's mind? We've made them think about the big service coming up. That might add some urgency. Now they may not know:

> 'Don't worry about that, leave it to us to find out. Is that service fully paid for?'

That might be a hook for a service plan if you sell that.

2. 'When's the MOT due? Anything that won't pass?'

> 'Mr or Mrs Customer, when is your NCT test due?' (Or, MOT certificate or roadworthy certificate...)

You'll be amazed how many people say it's only two or three months down the track, but don't leave it there. Ask the customer:

> 'Is there anything you think won't pass on that next test?'

They'll probably say no, but in their mind they'll be thinking about that chip on the windscreen or those ball joints. That adds a natural urgency.

3. 'When's the tax due?'

> 'Mr or Mrs Customer, when's the tax due?'

Plenty of people come in with a month or two left before the tax is due and that could be the catalyst for change.

> 'Just so you know, you'll get a cheque for any unspent tax back directly from the DVLA.'

You are both helping the customer and making them aware that they've got a tax bill coming up, and they've got some money they need to spend on their car soon. Dead money.

4. Tyres – maximum fine per tyre...

Tyres have 8mm on them when they're brand new. The legal limit in most European countries is 1.6mm (check with your local authority because Germany has a limit of 3mm). I hear the poor salesperson tell the customer, 'You've got 2mm on your tyres,' but there's no urgency there!

Do this instead. Get yourself a digital depth gauge to make it easy for the customer to read, then bend down and start measuring the depth of a tyre and say:

'Mr Customer, what sort of mileage are you doing a week? Really, 100km per week. Listen, just so you know, your two front tyres are worn way down, you've only got 0.4mm until they are illegal. To put that into perspective, that's the equivalent of the bumps on a credit card. Now the only reason I tell you that is because the government has changed the maximum fine to £2,500 per tyre and three points on your license. I'd hate for you to get pulled up by the police.'

Four great ways to add urgency. You're not delivering them as a threat – you're helping the customer. We are alerting the customer to what they might need to spend on the car and it might help create urgency.

Now we can have a look at the four opportunities to sell additional products.

Four bolt-ons

Your dealership might not sell all these bolt-ons, so just use the ones you do.

1. 'Where's the paint and fabric certificate?'

Start off by asking, 'Where's the paint and fabric certificate?' and you're looking for a, 'What's that?'

> 'That's a shame, my boss normally pays a touch extra when the customer's got the paint and fabric protection certificate, just because they know any scuffs or marks in the upholstery come straight back out, and it helps maintain that showroom shine when the car was brand new for the life of the vehicle. Check your paperwork because I'd be surprised if you don't have it. That's something a lot of my customers have.'

If they did buy the paint and fabric protection product last time, and we don't ask that question, you're telling the customer it's worthless. Sow the seeds early on.

2. 'What level of asset protection do you have?'

Now you can ask, 'What level of asset protection do you have on the car?' or 'What level of RTI or return to invoice protection do you have?' Again, you're looking for a, 'What's that?'

> 'That's something most of my customers have because everyone knows that insurance companies love to take the money but don't like paying it back out.'

3. 'Are you going to claim this scratch on the small repairs insurance?'

> 'Mr Customer, do you see the scuff on the side here? Do you want us to value the car as it is or will you claim on your motor vehicle insurance?'

Now everyone will say no, just value it as it is. Agree with the customer:

> 'I don't blame you, by the time you take into account your excess and what it does to your no claims bonus it's never worth doing. Or do you have that smart cover? Smart cover is something most of our customers have, effectively you have a pot of £3,000 you can spend over the next three years maintaining the showroom condition of your car. In fact, we can come out to you eighteen times to fix any scuffs or scratches up to 30cm in diameter or the thickness of a pound coin. You don't have anything like that, do you?'

4. 'Cash or finance?'

Most people borrow money for their car, but when you ask a customer how they're funding their car purchase, most people say cash! Why? Because people think they're going to get a better deal.

Don't just ask, 'How are you going to fund the new car?' We want to assume they're on finance because most people are. So, when we're looking at their car we ask:

> 'How many payments do you have left on your car?'
>
> Or
>
> 'When is your next payment due?'
>
> Or
>
> 'What's your guaranteed minimum future value?'

If we assume everyone has finance, it makes it easy for the customer to tell you the due date. If we say, 'Do you owe any money on it?' sometimes people's egos might talk and they say no, when in reality they're borrowing the money from the bank or building society. So, assume everyone's on finance.

To recap, when you look at the customer's car always take the customer with you, look at the four things for urgency, look at the four things for bolt-on products, and now, take the customer for a drive.

Say something along the lines of: 'I just need to take the car for a quick drive but for insurance purposes I need you to be in the car,' and when you're driving along, that's when we can ask the three famous questions:

> 'Mr or Mrs Customer, what do you like most about this car?'

Let them tell you what they really like, and listen.

> 'Is there anything that you haven't got on this car that you'd really like next time?'

Effectively I'm asking if there's anything they don't like about this car, but I suggest you don't use the words 'don't like' because you don't want them to feel bad about their previous purchase. And finally,

> **'Why are you looking to change?'**

Ask these questions while they are sitting in their car, in their comfort zone – and then we can use that qualified information to present the right feature to the right customer on the new car.

The best way to ask the customer what they want for their car? Don't!

This one's a little controversial. When I started in the motor trade, I was taught to ask a customer how much they wanted for their car early on in the process, and you might still have a manager or senior colleagues that always ask that question.

What's the advantage of asking someone how much they want for their car? They might tell you a price less than what the car's worth, but really you're just inviting people to give you a higher price. Customers have three prices in mind for their car:

1. The price they think is fair and would truly, honestly like.

2. A fairy-tale *asking* figure.

3. The amount they would ultimately *accept*.

So, let's say the car is worth £2,000: the customer would *really* like £2,500 but if we ask them what they were hoping to get for it, they're probably going to tell you £3,000. Now you've got a £1,000 difference to overcome. Or the customer has to take a £1,000 ego climbdown. If you ask the customer what they want for their car and they don't have a clue, you're forcing them to guess, and if they guess, they'll guess high!

There's another problem with asking people how much they want for their car – they'll turn around and say, 'You tell me, you're the expert', and right at the time we're trying to build rapport with the customer you can actually see them going back into their shell.

With all the research people do online, they have most certainly also found their current car for sale from lots of other independent buyers, other dealers or private people selling that car. When you ask them what they hope to get for it, even if they're honest with you, they'll give you a figure they've seen another retailer selling that car for. What they're not considering is that the dealer has had to get the car through a MOT, he's put two new tyres on it, he's providing a warranty for the next twelve months and then he wants a bit of margin!

If we don't ask the question and instead say, *'Great news, I've got some really good figures, the market value is £2,000'*, the customer might say, *'Hold on Simon, I really want at least £2,500'*. This is most likely the figure they'd really like and not a fairy-tale figure. The poor salesperson has a £1,000 difference to overcome. The smart salesperson only has a £500 problem to overcome. More deals are lost through saving face and the ego than by the actual money.

See 'OBJECTION 2: It's too expensive' and fairy-tale asking prices a little later for more ways to deal with this.

Never ask the customer how much they want for their car because you're inviting them to lie, guess, or call you out as the expert. You'll hear tricks about asking people when turning right into busy traffic how much they want. This trick may have worked twenty years ago because the only way a customer could get a price on the new car was to speak to us, the salespeople. And this technique only worked then because we'd asked earlier on in the process, and we knew they would tell us at least a thousand pounds over what the car was worth. Then our sales manager would work out what their car was worth, and the new car would suddenly get inflated by £1,000. We don't play these games anymore because every customer knows what the new car is worth anyway!

The presentation

> At no point in the history of time has anyone ever wanted a half inch drill bit, but every year thousands of half inch drill bits are sold. People didn't want a half inch drill bit, they wanted a half inch hole.

People don't actually want air conditioning, they want to stay nice and cool on the summer holiday drive down to Cornwall. People don't want climate control, they want to be able to set the temperature on different sides of the car to suit themselves or their partner. People don't want active lane departure warning systems, they want to stay safe or get cheaper insurance.

In this presentation we need to present the right feature to the right customer at the right time. That's why we looked at SPACER (Safety, Performance/Practicality, Aesthetics/Appearance, Comfort, Economy, Reliability) earlier, and about finding out what turns the customer on about that car so we know their

Gap. When we present the features, we need to make sure it's actually a presentation and not just a feature dump.

Remember the Feature-Advantage-Benefit strategy.

> **Feature**: This vehicle has the active lane departure warning system.

> **Advantage:** Which actively monitors the white lines on the road in front of you and steers the car back into the centre of the lane if you start swerving out of it.

> **Benefit:** So you and your family could be saved from death!

Putting it all together:

'Mr Customer, you're driving down the road, you know you shouldn't but you're looking down at Apple Play, or changing channels. You look up and you're actually half a metre into the other lane – thankfully no truck was there!

The beauty of this car, Mr Customer, is that it has the active lane departure warning system which actively monitors the white lines on the road in front of you and steers the car back into the centre of the lane. So if something like that happens the car is going to know that you're veering into the other lane and it's going to actively steer you back into the middle lane. It'll get you out of trouble before you're even in trouble.'

Joshua Bell is one of the leading classical violinists in the world, people pay a fortune for tickets to hear him play. In 2007 he went to Grand Central Station in New York and, wearing a baseball cap, he played the whole concert that he normally plays to sell-out audiences. But the presentation wasn't the same, and no one knew who he was. He played on the same $15 million Stradivarius violin, but no one knew who he was. 1,097 people walked past him and only twenty-seven gave him money. Only seven people stopped and listened for any length of time, and only one person noticed him. He got just $52.17, and $20 of that was from the person who recognised him.

What's the difference? The presentation. Take that man and put him in a concert hall, dress him in a tuxedo, and with the whole presentation people are willing to pay a hell of a lot more. Do the same for the car.

The Demonstration

Let's have a look at the demonstration drive. I'm deliberately calling it a demonstration drive and not a test drive because I don't believe test drives work anymore. In fact, I don't believe test drives ever worked. A test drive is what your technicians do to see if the car's working right. We need to demonstrate the right feature to the right customer at the right time.

We can do a lot of the presentation as part of the demonstration drive. Do bums in seats still sell cars? Yes, they always have, and I believe they always will.

How long should a demonstration drive be? Consider this: how long do you think it takes for someone to choose a pair of glasses at Specsavers? Not the eye test, just choosing a pair of glasses. I heard recently at a conference that it takes forty-eight minutes, on average, to choose the glasses. Now let's compare that to a demonstration drive. In 2017[1] the average demonstration drive in the UK was eleven minutes. Think about the difference of the cost of a pair of glasses versus a car. A pair of glasses costs a couple of hundred pounds at the top end, and people need forty-eight minutes of decision time. We're asking a customer to decide on a £20,000, £40,000, or even £60,000 car in eleven minutes. Most demonstration drives are too short. We know bums in seats sell cars. Who should drive the car first? I always recommend the salesperson drives the car first to take the opportunity to alternate the conversation between the car and the person. Something like:

'Hey, Mr Customer, one of the first things you'll notice about this car as I'm driving out of the dealership is that the steering is nice and light, that's because it's electronic power steering now, not hydraulic.

That hydraulic power steering on your car is spinning all the time, and what that's doing is taking power away from the engine and effectively fuel out of your tank. But this electronic power steering is only giving assistance when you need it. As my speed increases on this dual carriageway you'll notice the power steering becomes a little bit stiffer.

And for such a small car like this, you'll be impressed with how stable it is, because I know you said you go to Edinburgh regularly...'

1   Automotive Management Conference, 2017

Continue with something about the customer, then go back to demonstrating something about the car. Continue this on the drive out, find a lovely handover point, such as a golf course car park which are usually empty midweek. Then there are five things I want you to do when you get out of the car:

1. Put the seat back. I've got short little legs and I don't want a tall customer getting in and thinking the car is cramped.

2. Adjust the rear-view mirror. Avoid the customer feeling uncomfortable with a badly adjusted mirror by moving it so they have to adjust it perfectly for themselves. The more perfect it is, the better it's going to feel.

3. Reset the fuel trip metre. Every customer is interested in fuel consumption. I don't blame them, I am as well. So, reset the fuel trip computer now, not at the beginning of the journey, because internal combustion engines use more fuel warming up.

4. Set up the satellite navigation. Instead of you giving directions to the customer, let the sat nav do the work, while you concentrate on the customer.

5. Jump out with the keys. Some people take the keys out of the car so the customer doesn't steal it! This is very rare in the motor trade. The reason I take the keys is so that the customer doesn't drive the car until we have the chance to set up all the controls for them. Don't wait until you're sitting in the back of the car to show them the controls, show them while you're still in the driver's seat.

When they're driving the car, I want you to be quiet. There's magic in wrapping the metal around the people. Take care because if you've been chatting away and then you're suddenly quiet the customer might be concerned, so say: 'I'm just going to be quiet now and let the car sell itself. Any questions, feel free to ask.' Now I can shut up, and it's not an uncomfortable silence.

About five minutes before we get back to the dealership I'll start talking about mental ownership, get them into the yes frame of mind, try some trial closes. Let's talk about that in the next chapter.

Doubting the power of the demonstration drive

I teach negotiation for a living. I love selling skills, I love buying stuff from retailers and securing the best deal I possibly can. For fun I fly light aircraft and a few years ago I bought myself a new plane. Bearing in mind I train negotiation skills for a living, and quite frankly I think I'm pretty good at it, what discount do you reckon I got? Not a single penny. Guess what discount I asked for on the plane? Not a single penny. Why? The power of a demonstration done effectively.

I was driving home to Cheshire from London and I popped into Norfolk. I ran into a great salesperson who was talking about the plane, what it can do, fuel consumption and running costs, etc. He said, 'Do you know what, the weather's good, I'll take you out in mine and show you how great it is,' and he started pulling his plane out of the hangar. This ex-RAF Tornado pilot took me up, and we did some steep turns and some wing-overs – it was brilliant. He looked over at me, 'Good, isn't it?' Oh yes!

Then he said, 'Do you want one?' Oh yes! He then said, 'I've got one left in the container coming from Australia, should I put your name on it?'

'Yes please, that's mine. I've got to have one of these in my life.'

When we landed, he took me straight into the office, 'I'll just take £5,000 now to secure the order and then we'll talk about the exact specifications next week. That makes sense, doesn't it?'

I was on cloud nine driving back, and I was twenty minutes from home when I thought, 'Oh shit, I've got an Emma, and I never asked my wife. I never meant to go and buy a plane today. I'll just have to tell her I got a really good deal. Hold on, I didn't even ask for a discount!'

That's the power of a great demonstration. He got my emotions so high with his enthusiasm, I'd done the research before-hand (Norfolk's not on the way home from London) and everything else was secondary. Yes, you can sell a car without a demo. But why bother? It will just make your life so much harder.

Trial Close

Now we need to look at testing the customer's commitment to the product or service you are selling – or trial closing. Unless the product is right for them, it doesn't matter how cheap it is. That's why you must trial close before you *actually* close. All the trial close does is separate the product from the money.

We can do this in a few different ways. For example, at the end of the demonstration, when you're presenting the product, get them into that 'yes' frame of mind using the mental ownership technique.

Step One: 'That's going to make your life a lot easier, isn't it? It will be nice the next time you drive up to Scotland. How long does it take you to get there?'

Step Two: 'Have you driven the car far enough?'

Step Three: The trial close question. Here are a few options:

- 'If we can get the figures right, is this the car you'd like to own?'

- 'Apart from the figures, is there anything stopping you from wanting to own this car?'

- 'If everything stacks up right, is this the car you'd like to be driving for the next two or three years?'

Let's look at a few trial closes in more detail.

One simple question

'Apart from the figures, is there anything that's stopping you from wanting to own this car?'

The beauty of this one is that it's a simple question that's easy to remember. It also separates the product from the figures really well. But to get a positive outcome, the customer actually has to say no. And at this point, what we really want to do is get them into a yes frame of mind.

I find it works better if you turn the wording around: 'OK, Mr Customer, if we can get the figures right, is this the product you'd like to own?' Now, for a positive outcome, the customer has to say yes.

There might be another downside too. When you say 'apart from the figures', that might imply some sort of discounting. Some salespeople don't like it for that reason, so if you think it might be a problem try the next one instead.

Scale of one to ten

'Mr Customer, could you give me an indication – on a scale of one to ten – of how you rate this product overall?'

It doesn't matter what number they come back with, though it's surprising how often it's a seven or eight. So, then you say: 'Great! Sounds like we're just about on track. Can I ask you then, what would have to change to make it a perfect ten?' More often than not, the customer will say you will have to get the figures right.

The good thing about this one is that it identifies any objections. It's hard to close someone if they haven't 100% bought into the product and don't really feel that they want it.

Built-in mental ownership

Having said that, here's one I personally prefer: 'Overall this car is great – it will be so nice the next time you go to Scotland, won't it? Tell me, how long does it actually take to get there? OK. Well listen, if everything stacks up right, is this the car you'd like to be driving for the next two or three years?'

The reason I like this one is that mental ownership is built into the commitment question. You are going to get one of three responses:

1. 'Yes I really like it.'

In which case, you go straight into committing them. 'Great, so all we have to do is get the numbers right and that's the car you'd like to go ahead with?'

2. 'Well, not really.'

It doesn't matter what the actual objection is – the engine's too small, it's the wrong colour, whatever. The hardest objection to overcome is the one you don't know about. So, if you get a no, you either have to go back and present a slightly different product or... go on to the next response.

3. 'Well maybe, it could be.'

The wishie-washies. There's nothing else for it, you just have to go again: 'Mr Customer, when you say it "could be", it sounds like there's something you're not sure about. Is there something about the Holden Commodore that you're not 100% sure about?' By wording it like this, you're implying it's 99% right and only slightly wrong.

In my experience of selling, seven out of ten customers will say, 'No, it's really nice', so you can then go for a commitment by saying: 'Well, that just leaves the numbers side of it. If we can get that right, this is the car you'd like to be driving?'

Handling the smokescreen

What about the other three out of ten? You're going to get some kind of objection from them, but at this stage of the sales process it's likely to be minor – or even a smokescreen.

What do I mean by smokescreen? A few years ago, my wife and I were buying a house. We knew we'd found the one we wanted while the estate agent was showing us round, so naturally I started pointing out all the things I thought was wrong with it. Not because I didn't like the property, because I loved it. I was simply starting the negotiation stage early.

Yet a lot of salespeople, when they hear something like this, automatically think the product can't be right and start trying to sell the customer an alternative. Always remember that an objection at this point might be a smokescreen.

If it was a major objection, they would have flagged it up already – or rather, a good salesperson would have identified it. In the estate agent example, we wouldn't have got to the stage of looking round the house if it didn't have, say, the right number of bedrooms.

Similarly, if you show your customer a red car and they tell you they'd never drive one that colour, you're not going to get them out for a demonstration in it.

But, if later on in the sales process you trial close them by saying, 'So if everything stacks up right, is this the car you'd like to be driving for the next two or three years?' and they tell you they're not really sure about the colour, that is what I would say is a minor objection or smokescreen.

Minimise the objection

Minimise the objection by saying something like: 'OK, yes, well if everything stacks up right – the colour wouldn't stop you wanting to own it, would it?'

If they say, yes, it is going to stop them, you are just going to have to deal with it somehow. But at this stage of the process, after you've raised the desire, the vast majority of customers are going to say, 'No, not really'.

In life, we have to compromise all the time. Nothing's ever perfect. We didn't like everything about the house we bought, for example. But there were enough other things we really liked that made us think we could put up with the less than perfect parts.

That's why this technique is very good at either identifying the objection you've got to overcome, or confirming it's the product that they really want to own.

'Have you driven the car far enough?'

'Yes thanks'

'So, the car's nice, isn't it?'

'Yes lovely.'

'Great, so if everything stacks up right, is this what you'd like to be driving for the next two or three years?'

'Well, it could be...'

'OK, when you say "could be", it sounds like there's something you're not sure about. Is there something about the car that you're not 100% happy with?'

'Well, I'm not entirely sure about the wheels. I prefer the other one with the 19″ alloys to this one.'

'Yes, but if everything else stacks up right – the size of the wheels on it, that wouldn't stop you wanting to own this car, would it?'

'No, not really.'

'Great! It sounds like we have found the right car for you.'

That's when we're going to get to the commitment. You must ensure you get a commitment that the product or service is right before you start getting into any price negotiations or objection handling.

Ask the right question at the right time.

It's also a good idea to ask the commitment question when the customer is actually using the product. If it's a suit, ask them while they're still wearing it. Don't wait until they've taken it off again. If it's a house, ask them when they are actually in it. If it's a holiday, ask them when it's still showing on the screen.

Final Close

How can you close more sales? If you're anything like me, you've flicked straight through to this chapter! But if you have, go back and read the rest first. Because the real key to closing is opening up the sale properly in the first place.

As we've discussed, you need to meet and greet the customer, open them up and get them into your sales process, qualify their wants and needs, and identify a problem with their current situation that you can offer a solution to. You've got to present your product or service to raise the desire, and you have to demonstrate how your product is going to help them. Then you test their commitment with a trial close question.

'So, Mr Customer, if everything else stacks up right, is this the product you'd like to own?' Or,

'So, apart from the figures, is there anything stopping you from wanting to own this one?'

Questions such as these herald the start of the closing stage. Let's look first at some ground rules for this point in the sales process.

1.   You need to be confident. This is where the trial close pays dividends. Your trial close ensures the product is right for the customer, and allows you to go into your close with poise and self-assurance.

2. Maintain eye contact. If you've ever spoken to someone who was wearing mirrored sunglasses, you'll know how off-putting it can be when you can't see their eyes. For example, if you're with a customer and you're talking about something on the spec sheet or some other piece of paper, come back up and make eye contact. Don't just focus on the paperwork all the time, because if customers can't see your eyes, there will be less trust there.

   And if you live in a hot country, or it's a particularly bright summer's day, be sure to take the sunglasses off!

3. Present the price, or the deal, to the customer and ask how – not if – they want to go ahead.

Be careful with your wording as well. If you are saying to customers things like, 'So, what are your thoughts?' or 'What do you think?' – what's the last word you have left in the customer's head? It's 'think', as in '… I need to go away and think about it.' Who's causing the problem here – us or them?

Look at the fast-food industry, where they ask you what size of drink you want – small, medium or large? The last word left in the customer's head? 'Large'. By the same token, I stay in hotels quite a lot and often, at the end of the evening, I'll ask for a glass of red wine.

'Large?'

'Oh, go on then.'

Be aware of the words you plant in your customers' heads; try to avoid asking them 'what do you think?', not least because of rule number one – be confident. There's no confidence in asking customers what they think.

The Direct Close

The Direct Close is great for the lion. What is the best way to ask these customers how they want to proceed? The most obvious way is the Direct Close, where you simply ask them:

'Shall we go ahead with that?'

'Shall we secure that for you?'

'Shall we get that ordered for you?'

I personally like 'secure'. Customers love security in their lives. It means that what they have bought is theirs and nobody else's – and that's especially important in the housing market, for example.

There's a risk with the Direct Close, however, and it's not the one you might be thinking of – that the customer can only answer either yes or no. That is the case with any kind of closing technique. The real risk here is that for your customer it might be too blunt. If you have built up a good rapport with them and they like you, they might be unwilling to tell you that they don't like something about your product or service.

Now, I'm going to be controversial for a moment. I don't believe the true purpose of a closing question is to actually close the sale. Instead, it's to draw out or uncover the objection that you know you will inevitably get. The way you *actually* close the sale is by overcoming that objection, which we'll look at in the next section. That's the real key to closing.

The alternative close

A good closing question will assume the customer wants to go ahead. So, try the alternative close sometimes as well, where you give the customer two choices – either of which is equally good for you.

> 'Mr Customer, did you want to go ahead with that by financing it over thirty-six months, or is it more comfortable for you over forty-eight months?'

Or:

> 'Did you want to pick this up on Thursday, or would Friday be better for you?'

The reason this works is because if ever we are asked a question, the human mind cannot help but answer it – even if only internally. Let me try and prove it to you, while you are reading this book. Have you ever been in a light aircraft? Ridden a motorbike? Been to Australia? Do you find yourself saying yes or no to these questions? You can't help it, it's an instinctive response.

When you ask your customers if they want to pick it up next Thursday or Friday, straight away they are going to be thinking about which one they'd prefer.

That's why the alternatives close works really well. They've got two choices, but you don't mind which one it is.

The couple close

The Couple Close is great for the puppy dog. If you have a couple together – a husband and wife, or maybe even business partners – ask them this: 'Listen, whose name are we going to put the paperwork in? Joint names, or just one of you?'

Then step back and wait for one of them to pipe up with 'well, it is my car', or whatever the product or service happens to be. It doesn't matter to you whose name it's in, so let one of their egos do your selling for you.

The summary close

This one is a variation of a children's game, and is great for the mouse or snake. It's where you have a few little yeses to get to the one big yes. You've probably done this with your own children, or remember it from school:

'What's the colour of the pages in this book?' 'White!'

'What's the name of the US President's house?' 'The White House!'

'What do cows drink?'

It's surprising how many people say milk... when of course the answer is water!

In a sales context, you can achieve the same effect by simply going back over your qualification, and where the 'big yes' is assumptive. Here's an example for a different industry:

'Mr Customer, you wanted three bedrooms, which we've got for you. You wanted it close to the school and you're in the catchment area. You wanted to move before Easter, and we could have you in here on 10 March. There's the home office space and room at the back to kick a football around. You wanted to keep the budget to around £350,000, and we are there or thereabouts. It sounds like we've got the right house for you.'

The 'big yes' here is the assumptive, 'Sounds like we've found the right one for you.' Reach for a handshake as well when you say it, to try and secure that commitment.

Salespeople often tell me they fear holding their hand out when they are looking for commitment at the end of a sale, in case the customer doesn't take it. What if you're just left hanging?

Well, what if you are? It's happened to me in probably half of my sales. In fact, the very last time I sold a car before writing this section I had to offer my hand four times before the customer would take it. That's the real world. When a customer leaves you hanging, use it to identify their objection. Like this:

> 'OK, you're not taking my hand there, I must have missed something? Can I ask you, Mr Customer, is there one of these figures you're not 100% sure about?'

Then you are back to your objection handling techniques. Don't be afraid to stick out your hand when you ask a closing question. Be confident.

The Assumptive Close

All the closing questions we have looked at so far have been assumptive. You have already trial closed, you know they want the product and that it's right for them, and to close them you can just start running through all the things they'll need.

You might be presenting a new website to a client, or a sales training programme for example. Don't just ask them 'so, do you want to go ahead then?'

Talk about the things the customer needs to do: 'Mr Customer, we're going to need your licence from you, we're going to need this and that, and we're also going to need £1,000 to secure it. Do you want to put that on a credit or debit card?'

It's not a question of *if* they want to go ahead – you just assume they do.

In fact, when I'm selling sales training, it's often the close that I use. It's not *if* we are going to go ahead and do the work with you, it's *when*.

'You'll want this started, I take it, either just after the busy September new car plate-change month – or well before. So, listen, we could start the week beginning the 14th, or would the following week be better?' That's a true Assumptive Close.

The Conditional Close

'If I could... would you... ?'

If it's important for the customer to get a quick delivery, you can use this one as a closing technique:

> **'If I can get that for you by the 16th of next month, shall we go ahead with it?'**

Or:

> **'If I could get you that extra £500 for your part exchange, can we go ahead with it?'**

It works very well because it satisfies the first fundamental of selling – the fundamental of comparison.

There must be literally thousands of other closes. But they all come down to asking for a commitment to go ahead with your product or service.

Shut Up!

To recap, the main keys to closing more customers are:

- Be confident

- Present the price and maintain eye contact

- Present the deal and use one of the closing techniques listed in this section

- Then stop talking. You may have heard this before, but he who talks first loses. I hate the thought of someone buying a product as 'losing', but to be fair there is some truth in it

All too often, though, I hear salespeople shutting up at the wrong moment. They present their figures to the customer, and wait for them to speak – without asking one of the closing questions first.

What tends to happen then is that you get an uncomfortable silence. And customers invariably fill it by saying to you something like: 'Well, that is certainly food for thought, thank you. Now we really need to go away and think about it.'

Don't shut up until you've asked the customer how they want to go ahead with it. 'Do you want pick it up next Thursday, or would the weekend be better?' That's when you should go quiet – and offer a handshake.

Those, then, are the rules for effective closing. Now, I can hear what you're thinking – it's not going to work every time. And no, it won't. A lot of the time you're going to uncover an objection – they want more of a discount, they've seen a better one somewhere else, they want to go away and think about it.

We're going to look at the different ways of overcoming the objections you come up against most often in the following section.

Overcoming Objections

Customers can throw in an objection at any point in the sales process, but I want to focus on the objections you get once you start negotiating with them. I hear a lot of sales trainers saying that objections arise because you haven't qualified the customer properly, and undoubtedly that is often the case. But I also believe we sometimes qualify the customer almost *too* well.

If you've built up a lot of rapport, and the customer likes you, they might not feel comfortable telling you they just don't like your product or service. So instead, they say they want to go away and think about it. And that, as we all know from experience, is just another way of saying, 'No way am I ever going to buy this!'

You probably also get your share of customers who tell you they've been offered a better deal from somebody else down the road. Again, that might be true, but it's just as likely to be code for, 'Can you do me a better deal?'

Let's look at the objections that salespeople typically face every day. Remember there are three sales that have to happen with every sale – because if you're getting a lot of objections to price, chances are you are focusing too much on selling the deal. You've got to sell yourself first and then the product before you sell the deal.

OBJECTION 1: 'I Want to Think About It'

What do you do when you're trying to close a customer and they tell you they want to go away and think about it? You've spent a bit of time with them, given them a demonstration, asked a couple of trial close questions and got a degree of commitment from them. Things are looking good. So you put a deal in front of them, but they say: 'Well, it's a big decision for us, you don't buy a car every day. I want to make sure it's the right one.'

More often than not, you know they've got some kind of objection – you're just not sure what it is. Because customers don't really go away and 'think about it', they end up buying somewhere else.

What do you do? In the past, I used to say, 'Well, what do you want to think about?' But it doesn't really work. A lot of customers see it as too confrontational and you end up losing the sale. The answer is to find out what their true objection is by getting them to open up. Then at least you've got a chance of overcoming it while they're there. To do that, we need to find a different way of asking, 'What do you want to think about?'

These word tracks are designed to be non-confrontational, and to take the pressure off the customer. Only use them after you've presented a deal to the customer, trial closed them and got some degree of commitment from them. They won't work if you haven't built a good rapport with your customer first. That is where a lot of salespeople go wrong – moving too quickly to the close. Here are some word tracks to the objection: 'I want to think about it.'

If only...

> 'Sure, I understand that. Buying a car is a big decision and shouldn't be taken lightly. Here's my business card, here are the brochures, if you have any questions please give me a call.'

It's important to start by acknowledging their position. This will take the pressure off the customer, which usually causes them to open up a little.

> 'But I'd hate to think that you leave here, get up to the traffic lights at the end of the road and turn to one another and say, "If only he did such and such, we would have bought that". Just so you don't have to have that conversation, while you're here, can I ask you – what would that something be?'

Scale of one to ten

This technique comes from David Martin. David is one of the great sales trainers in the motor industry. He has been voted Best Speaker at the National Automotive Dealers Association (NADA) and I'm proud to have a joint training venture with him and the Markee group. This is one of David's signature techniques.

'Sure, I understand that. Buying a new car is a big decision and shouldn't be taken lightly. Here's my business card, here are the brochures, if you have any questions please give me a call.

'But please, could you give me an indication of how you rate it overall, on a scale of one to ten – ten being that's the car you'd like to be driving for the next ten years; and one being it's not the right one for you at all. How would you rate it?'

Most people will give you a seven to a nine, but the number doesn't matter. Whatever they say, come back with: 'OK, sounds like we're on track. But can I ask you, what would have to change to make that a perfect ten?'

I buy things as well

'Sure, I understand that. Buying a new car is a big decision and shouldn't be taken lightly. Here's my business card, here are the brochures, if you have any questions please give me a call. But you know what, I buy things all the time as well. And whenever I've told a salesperson I want to think about it, it's usually because there's something I'm not sure about and I just don't want to offend them. Is there something about the car, or perhaps our figures here, that you are not 100% sure about, and you just don't want to offend me?'

Three questions

'Sure, I understand that. Buying a car is a big decision and shouldn't be taken lightly. Here's my business card, here are the brochures, if you have any questions please give me a call. But you know, no matter how long you want to think about it, it always comes back to three questions: is this the car you'd like to be driving for the next few years; are we the people you feel comfortable doing business with; and do the figures fit into the budget you were hoping to achieve?

'So, can I ask you, is that the car you'd really like to be driving?'

It's going to be a yes, because you've already trial closed them.

'Are we the people you feel comfortable doing business with?'

Who is going to say no to that? If they do, you have a major problem!

'So that just leaves the figures. Can I ask you, which figure here are you not 100% sure about? Is it this one here, this one here, or one of these?'

I tend to use this one on customers who give you a time-frame: 'Give me the weekend to think about it,' or 'What time do you close? We'll let you know then.'

The couple

> 'Sure, I understand that. Buying a new car is a big decision and shouldn't be taken lightly. Here's my business card, here are the brochures, if you have any questions please give me a call. But listen, I've just had a thought. Let me go and quickly check with the boss about something.'

Then leave. Go and check on stock availability or something. Don't say: 'Would you like me to make you a coffee while you talk about it here,' because they will always come back with something like, 'No thanks, we want to go away and think about it.'

You'll be amazed how many times, when you come back to the customer, they say: 'It's just the colour, I'm not sure we can live with that,' or 'We really wanted one with the x feature.'

Trial close

> 'Sure, I understand that. Buying a car is a big decision and shouldn't be taken lightly. Here's my business card, here are the brochures, if you have any questions please give me a call. But listen, when we took the car for a drive, you did say that if we could keep the figures right, it's the car you'd like to own. So, it sounds like I haven't got one of these figures exactly right for you. Can I ask you, which figures here are you not 100% sure about? This one, this one, or one of these?'

A lot of people don't like this technique. It can seem too hard with the customer. But is it? You've spent a fair bit of time with them, so don't you have the right to ask what's stopping them from going ahead? Bounce it back to the trial close.

Your mates

> 'Sure, I understand that. Buying a car is a big decision and shouldn't be taken lightly. Here's my business card, here are the brochures, if you have any questions please give me a call. But listen, in half an hour's time, when you're having a beer with your mate in the pub, and you tell him how good that new car is, when he asks you why you didn't buy it, what are you going to say?'

You need to be confident and have a good rapport with your customer for this one to work, so be selective about which ones you use it with.

For instance, if it's an elderly customer you could say: 'But listen, in half an hour's time, when you're talking with family and friends about how good that new car is, when they ask you if you're going to get it, what are you going to say?'

Or, for the business customer: 'In half an hour's time, when you're back in the office talking to your colleagues about the Audi, and how good it is, when they ask you if you're you going to go ahead and order it, what's the answer you're going to tell them?'

First choice

Here's an example from a different industry to show you the flexibility of the track.

> Customer: 'Thanks very much. I really like your Nikon, and I think I'm going to go ahead with it. But I just need to go and look at the Canon, to put it out of my mind.'
>
> **'Sure, I understand that. Buying a camera is a big decision and shouldn't be taken lightly. But I think what you're saying is, what is it that made the Nikon your first choice – the camera you wanted to see first? Why it's most people's first choice is because it's the best in its class. It was probably your first choice because it's got the autofocus system on it that you said you really wanted. It's got the capacity to shoot HD video, which was important to you as well. It's got the dual memory card slot, etc, etc. Isn't it worth buying the camera that's your first choice?'**

Whatever you do, don't start rubbishing your competitor's product. It's counter-productive, because the customer will – in their own mind at least – start defending it and re-selling it to themselves.

With this one, if you don't close the sale, you're at least letting them leave with all their 'hot buttons' reinforced.

John's choice

> 'I just need to go and see the Audi first, to put it out of my mind.'
>
> **'You're just like my wife!'**
>
> 'Sorry?'
>
> **'Just like my wife. Say she wants a new pair of shoes. So, on my one day off we go to the Trafford Centre. We go into one shop and she finds a pair she likes. Does she buy them? No, she spends the rest of my day off going to every shop in the mall – and guess which ones she ends up buying?'**
>
> 'The first?'
>
> **'Exactly. Isn't it worth getting the car that's your first choice?'**

Again, if you don't have a really good rapport with your customer, don't even think about using this one!

By the way, it's called John's Choice because I saw it in a Toyota dealership and that was the salesperson's name. It worked really well for him!

OBJECTION 2: It's Too Expensive

The most common objection that tends to come up is price. You present the product, the customer likes it, but then they say it's too much. A lot of salespeople tend to jump in at this point and say something to the effect of: 'So where do we need to be then?'

There's a big problem with this. Say your product is £9,995. Remember, these sales tracks can be applied to any big-ticket items, it could be anything – a kitchen or bathroom, computer or audio equipment, service contracts, sales training programmes, etc. First, you need to remember that as customers we have three prices in our mind when we're shopping:

1. The price we think is fair and would like to pay (let's say in this case it's £9,500).

2. A fairy-tale figure that we ask for initially (let's say £10,000).

3. The amount we would ultimately be prepared to pay if we have to (£9,750).

As salespeople, what we need to do is prise that first 'liking' figure out of the customer's head and onto the table, and eliminate their fairy-tale asking figure altogether.

Think about it. If the customer rejects your initial offer and asks you how much further you can go, by going straight into 'where do we need to be?' you are simply telling them there is indeed some room for manoeuvre on your part.

All the rapport and trust you have built up over the last hour, week or more can be lost in an instant – as a result of revealing that you haven't yet put your best deal down. In fact, you could be creating a shopper right there.

So, avoid going straight into 'where do we need to be?'

It's a mistake I used to make often. I'd offer a car at £9,995, the customer would baulk, and when I asked him where we needed to be, he'd give me his fairy-tale figure of £9,000.

'So, if I could do it for that would you buy it today?' I would ask. He would indeed. So, I'd go and tell my sales manager.

'He'll buy it today for £9,000, boss!' To which the boss would reply: 'I'm sure he would, and so would I! Now get back out there and tell him we can do it for £9,800.'

You can see the problem. Because I'd invited him to say £9,000, this was the figure he had in his head and would be expecting us to meet somewhere in the middle. That's why we need to get customers talking to us about their true 'liking' figure, not their fairy-tale asking figure.

Justify your offer

Here's how to handle that price objection more effectively. The first step is justifying your offer. That means going back to all the things the customer said they liked about your product or service – their hot buttons, in other words.

> 'That surprises me, Mr Customer. Getting the money side of it right is usually the easiest part of my job. We're one of the biggest dealers in the area, we sell more Volvos than anyone else I know, and that's because we're competitive to start with. Also bear in mind, the car you are buying has the air-con you said you really wanted, the leather seats, the sat nav, etc, etc.'

Having justified your offer, you can then start conditioning the customer and hopefully bring a more realistic figure into play.

> 'Having said that, we might have a bit of room to move. Realistically, what were you hoping to pay for a 2018 plate XYZ with air-con, satnav, and leather interior – £9,900? £9,800? Something like that?'

Now you're putting some parameters around the counter offer. Now, no customer is going to turn around and say: 'Oh all right then, £9,900.' But what it does do is get this fairy-tale figure out of the way. You're probably going to hear a reply along the lines of: 'No, I really don't want to pay more than £9,500.'

Now you are more likely to end up agreeing to a deal somewhere between your own asking price and the customer's true liking figure.

> 'Realistically, what were you hoping to pay for that, £9,900? £9,800? Something like that?'

The word 'realistically' is very powerful. I interviewed a salesperson not long ago, and I asked how much he was looking to earn over the next twelve months. Without missing a beat, he said £50,000. I said: *'Realistically?'* Just one word, but straight away he came back with: 'Well, at least £30k.' One word potentially saved me £20,000 there!

Conditioning the customer

This sort of conditioning happens in all walks of life. And if you're not conditioning the customer, they are probably conditioning you.

Many years ago, I went home to Australia for a friend's wedding with a six-month old baby. After a twenty-four-hour flight, all we wanted to do was go to the wedding, do the reception and then sneak away. But the best man came up and conditioned me.

'Simon,' he said, 'We're booking taxis for later on, shall we get one for you as well?'

'Yes, thanks, that would be great.'

Then he conditioned me by saying: 'What time should I book it for? 12.30? 1.00? Something like that?' Did I tell him 9 o'clock, which was when we wanted to go, or did he drag me out a bit later?

'Listen, we're tired and jetlagged, any chance you could book it for 11?'

'Sure Simon, no problem!'

I told Emma we were going home at 11, and she said: 'But I thought we were leaving at 9?'

'I know! I was conditioned.'

Feasible and flexible

Let's go back to our earlier example of the car we were selling at £9,995, where the customer has said: 'No, I don't want to pay more than £9,500.'

I was taught to respond with: 'We can't do it at £9,500. What would you buy it at?'

The trouble with this, though, is that if you tell anyone they can't do something, their natural reaction is to want to prove you wrong. That's why the word 'can't' is one to avoid. As is 'buy' (download our Words to Avoid extra chapter from the website to find out why).

> So, let's swap them for two different words – **'feasible'** and **'flexible'**. If you only learn two words from this book, these will make it worth your while.

'You're kidding? £2,990? I want it for less than that!'

'Only two-grand for my part exchange? I need more than that!'

That's the sort of thing salespeople hear all the time, not just in the car trade but across all sales environments. Here's how to counter it:

> 'That surprises me, Mr Customer. Getting the money right on part exchanges is usually the easiest part of my job. Please bear in mind, that £2,000 for your car – it's because there are a couple of new tyres needed and you've got a scuff down the side.
>
> Having said that, we might have a bit of room to move. Realistically, what were you hoping to get for your car? £2,100? £2,200? Something like that?'
>
> 'No, I need at least £2,500.'
>
> 'Looking at the money that's going to be spent on your car, I just don't think £2,500 is going to be feasible. How flexible can you be?'

You will probably find the 80/20 rule kicks in here. I find that around 80% of my customers say something like:

'What do you mean by flexible?' or 'How flexible?' Or,

'When you say flexible, what exactly do you mean?'

What they're really saying here is: 'Pick me up by the ankles, shake me really hard, and more money's going to fall out of my pocket.' Let's explore that.

'OK, we see the market value at £9,950 and we've priced it very competitively, because in the modern world we have to be competitive on the internet – just to get people to want to come in and look at our range. Because of that, we don't have a huge margin on top that we can just knock off. Having said that, we might have a little bit of room to move. Realistically, what were you hoping to get it for? £9,900? £9,800? Something like that?

'We don't want to go above £9,500 really.'

'OK, look, just for an 19-plate XYZ, it's got this on it, this on it and that on it, I just don't think £9,500 is going to be feasible. How flexible can you be?'

'What do you mean?'

'Well, the market value is at £9,995 and you'd like £9,500. Where in the middle could we meet?'

'Well, it's got to be at least £9,750.'

Now we've got them to £9,750, we're going to try and commit them.

'So, what you are saying, Mr Customer, is if I could do that for £9,750, you'd be happy to shake my hand. Is that right?'

It's the conditional close that we highlighted previously.

Third party negotiation

Leave the customer alone for a moment while you seek confirmation. Don't just give up the extra money straight away, even if you know you've got that extra £250 up your sleeve, or they may well think it was there for them all along.

'Let me go and check with my boss.'

'Let me go and check with my supplier.'

'Let me go and check with someone.'

This technique is called third party negotiation. It's a good one to add to your armoury because if you are the person who denies them the extra discount it will be you they don't like. But if it's your boss who won't give it to them, then it's him or her they don't like. Would you deal with a business where you didn't like the salesperson? Maybe you would – but probably only if it was ultra-cheap.

Good news – we're close

So, you've gone away to check and now you've come back. The final stage is where you tell the customer: 'Good news, we're close.' Then shut up and listen. You will get one of three reactions:

1. They will lean across the desk and say: 'How close?' What they are really telling you here is that they really want it and may be willing to pay more than they agreed. 'Well OK, we can do that at nine-eight for you.'

2. You give them the 'good news' and they come back with: 'If it's not £9,750 don't even bother,' which allows you to reply: 'Yes, my boss is just making another phone

call. Do you want another coffee while you're waiting?'
Effectively, all we've done here is tested the water,
before we show our hand.

3. Finally there are the people in the middle. 'Go on then,
   what do you mean by close?' These are the people to
   whom you might not give the full £250. You have to
   make a judgment based on the customer's reaction.

To recap, there are three steps to this technique:

'You're kidding? Two-grand? I need more than that for my part exchange.'

'Well that surprises me, Mr Customer, we never usually miss a deal by that much. Getting the money right is normally the easiest part of my job. We're one of the biggest groups in the area and we didn't get to be that way by getting our figures wrong. Having said that, we might have a little bit of room to move. Realistically, what were you hoping to get for that? £2,100? £2,200? Something like that?'

'No, I need at least £2,500.'

'Well with the tyres so low and that scrape on your car, I just don't think £2,500 is going to be feasible. How flexible can you be?'

'What do you mean, flexible?'

'Well, my boss sees the market value of your car at £2,000 and we work within a market – we don't create the market. You'd like £2,500. Where in the middle could we meet?'

'It's got to be £2,300, really.'

'So what you're saying is that if I could pay you £2,300 for your car, which makes that a £7,700 balance, you'd like to go ahead with it. Is that right?'

'Yes.'

'The reason I say that is, I'm going to need that extra £300 from an independent buyer. So, if I can get that, you will want to go ahead with it, won't you?

'Yes.'

'Great, I'll see what we can do!'

Then you go away – but don't come straight back in to say 'yes, we can do it.' Even at this stage, they will know it was up your sleeve all the time. If you give any extra money, you need to give a reason why.

Make them feel like they've worked a good deal

It's basic negotiation. Always reduce the amount you go back with. Say the price of your product is £900, and the customer declines. If you then go back in at £850, then £800, then £750, etc, a lot of your customers will keep saying no if they know that every time they do that you are going to take another £50 off.

Instead, keep reducing the amount of the discount. If you start at £900 and then got to £850, if the customer is still holding out you should offer £825 and then £810. You are going to end up with more profit in your deals, but more importantly your customers will feel like they've worked a good deal.

OBJECTION 3: 'I Can Get It Cheaper Somewhere Else'

Say the product or service you are selling is £10,000. The customer says they can get it for less elsewhere. When they tell you they can get the same product or service you're selling for less somewhere else, instinctively you'll want to ask them how much. But is that a good idea? You might be just inviting a lie.

If you're asking £9,995 and they say they can get it for £9,000, you might offer them £9,500. But here's the trouble: even if your offer is better than what they've actually been offered, you have a face-saving problem to contend with. If your customer can't buy from you without losing face, they've got to back their lie up.

A cautionary tale

A few years ago, I was about to become a father and I wanted to buy a digital video camera to record our son growing up. So naturally I shopped around first, to satisfy my need for comparison.

I went to a retail park where they had a Comet, a Curries, and Scottish Power almost side-by-side. I didn't really know what I wanted so I went into the first one, spoke to a salesperson, looked at a few different models and narrowed it down to a particular Sony. So then I asked him: 'What's your best price?'

'Sir,' he said, 'our prices are permanently low.'

I tried but I just couldn't budge him. He offered to throw in a set of digital video tapes, but that was as far as he was prepared to go.

So, I went to the next store, told the salesperson what I wanted and asked him: 'What's your best price?'

He wanted to know if I would be taking the extended warranty, which I wouldn't, and again he wouldn't budge on the price beyond a few free video tapes. The price was virtually identical to the previous store at around £500, maybe £5 cheaper.

I went to the third store where it was actually about £10 more expensive. 'Hold on a minute,' I said, 'I can get that cheaper elsewhere.'

'That's fine sir,' the salesperson replied. 'We have a price match promise. We guarantee to match the price if it's cheaper anywhere else. How much did you see it for?'

Straight away I was wondering, what's the margin on one of these things? If I go too low he's just going to tell me to go away and buy it elsewhere. But if I'm too high, I'm going to be doing myself out of a deal. So, I blurted out £450.

'No problem sir,' he said, 'if you'd like to come with me to the counter, I'll get that sorted for you. How would you like to pay for it?'

'I'll put it on my debit card, thanks!' That was easy, I thought. Almost too easy! We got to the counter, where he asked me where I saw it and how much it was for.

That's when it started to unravel. He picked up the phone, dialed, paused, and then said: 'Hi Bob, it's Charlie. How's things? Yes, pretty busy too. Listen, the Sony Model Ref No… how much are you guys selling that for? £497? Really? It's just that I've got a customer here who told me it was £450. Can you check with your manager that you haven't done one at £450 today? You're quite sure? Ah, OK then, he must be mistaken.'

The mistake this salesman made? He'd caught me on a bare-faced lie! How embarrassed was I now? But here's the thing, he lost the sale. I couldn't bring myself to buy from him. In fact, every time I walked past there again, I felt I couldn't even go in because I was still so embarrassed. I couldn't buy the camera from the store he'd just phoned either, which was the cheapest. I had to go to the one in the middle.

The mistake the salesman made here was forcing me to back my lie up. Of course, he had a war story to tell. You can picture him in a huddle with the other staff at lunchtime: 'You'll never believe the muppet I had this morning. I sure taught him…' I'm not denying, as a salesperson, that that's a good feeling. So why not do it once in a while, just for the pleasure of it? But just be aware that whenever you catch a customer out like that, you won't be closing the sale.

A better way that results in a sale

So, what's a better way of dealing with situations like this? How do you overcome the objection when customers tell you they can get it cheaper elsewhere? Try an approach based on the following word track:

'You know, that surprises me, Mr Customer. We're one of the biggest dealers in the area and we didn't get to be that way by getting our figures wrong. We don't have massive overheads, and getting the figures right is usually the easiest part of my job.'

That's the first stage – justify your offer. Then follow it up with something along the lines of: 'If all things were equal, if the figures were there or thereabouts, where would you really prefer to buy from?'

Your approach should be slightly different depending on whether it's an identical product of the same brand or a similar product from a different supplier. Let's say it's the latter. The customer tells you it is cheaper elsewhere. Think it through. For a start, if they really prefer this other vehicle, then why are they sitting in front of you now? Try something like this:

> 'Mr Customer, that surprises me. Getting the money right is usually the easiest part of my job. We sell more XYZs than anyone else I know in the area, and that's partly because we price them so competitively to start with. But tell me, if everything was equal, if the figures were there or thereabouts, which one would you really prefer to own?'

It's something of a gamble, but nine times out of ten they are going to say yours – because they're in front of you. That allows you to paint them into a corner by asking: 'Really? Why's that?'

You're going to hear things like, 'Well, yours has got air-con and the leather interior' or, 'Yours is a lovely shade of silver; theirs was in doom blue' or, 'Yours has 40,000 miles on the clock, the other one had 45,000.'

Whatever they say, agree with them!

'Yes, Mr Customer, I can understand that. I would prefer to buy the car with air-con as well – because it's not just the next three years of driving in comfort. Any money you save now on a car without air conditioning, you will only lose later when you decide to trade it in.'

Or: 'Yes, I can understand that, Mr Customer, I'd prefer to buy a car with 60,000 miles on it rather than 90,000 – because with that 90,000-mile car you're going to have to get that cam belt done before you even think about changing. Any money you save now will only cost you later. So, if you could just be a little flexible, I'm going to see if my boss can be flexible too – and I'm going to get you into the car you would really prefer to own.'

Here's why this is important. All too often, when a customer says they can get the same car for cheaper elsewhere, we ask: 'Is it the same car? Are we comparing apples with apples here?' They will almost certainly say yes, if only to get you to drop your price. And in this situation, it's three strikes against you and you're out.

> **'Is it the same model?'**
> 'Yes'
> **'Same mileage?'**
> 'Lower!'
> **'Same colour?'**
> 'Nicer!'
> **'Same spec?'**
> 'Better!'

Where do you go from there? You're in a funny place called Stuck!

Get them to sell it to themselves

Now, what if it's an identical product of the same brand?

'You know, that surprises me, Mr Customer. Getting the money right is usually the easiest part of my job. Tell me, if all things were equal, if the figures were there or thereabouts, which laptop would you really prefer to own?'

When they say, 'Oh, definitely this one,' ask them why. Because by doing this, you're getting your customers to sell it to themselves. That is the key.

It's the same if you're a salesperson selling services. I use this in my business all the time. We're not the cheapest sales training company, and don't ever want to be. In fact, we want to be the most expensive, because that's how we make our profit. When someone says we are dearer than some other vendor, every sinew in my body wants to ask them how much they're doing it for. But if I say that, what are the chances of them telling the truth? Am I not simply inviting a lie?

What I say instead is this: '

> 'That surprises me. Getting the finance side of it right is normally the easiest part of my job – because we make sure we are very competitive in the marketplace all the time. So, can I ask you, Mr Customer, if all things were equal, if the figures were there or thereabouts, which training company would you really prefer to use?'
>
> 'Oh, definitely yours.'
>
> 'Really, why's that?'
>
> 'Well, you guys have got that hands-on approach – a real world approach and the Sales Fitness training videos to back up the initial training.'

Can you see how you are getting the customer to say they prefer your product?

'Yes, I understand that, I would prefer that hands-on approach too. Because that's where your salespeople, when they see things actually being done, will put in place changes that lead to long-term improvement. If you can just be a little bit flexible, I'll speak to Darren, our Sales Director – and see if we can be a touch flexible too. And we'll try and get you the training package you'd really prefer. Is that fair enough?'

The final stage

The final stage is to find out how much they think they can get it for elsewhere – but by conditioning them and putting some parameters around the counter offer.

'Listen, how much are they doing that product down the road for? What, £9,900, £9,800, something like that?' Or,

'How much are they doing that for as a part exchange? What, £7,850, something like that?' Or,

'How much are they doing that a month for? £290, £280, something like that?'

The point of conditioning them is to try and establish the true amount, not some fairy-tale figure.

All this is designed to stop the lie, or at least reduce the amount of the lie.

EIGHT

Waypoint 4: Follow Up

How Soon Is Too Soon?

OK, you've been through the sales process, spent time with the customer and done everything right. But then they tell you they want to go away and think about it – and there is simply nothing you can do to turn them around. When do you follow them up? It's a question I often put to salespeople, and they often tell me they leave it a week, or two to three days.

In the internet age, that's far too long. If you've done a trial close and made sure the product was right before you started talking prices, you can be fairly certain it's price your customer is thinking about. And because of the fundamental of comparison, they're going to want to shop around.

My concern is that once they've left your premises, one of them will turn to the other and ask them what they think. The conversation then runs something like this:

> **'I loved it.'**
>
> 'So did I.'
>
> **'Shall we get it then?'**
>
> 'Yes let's.'

That's just about the worst conversation that can happen, because only very rarely will they actually turn around and come straight back. Instead, it's more likely to end with one of them saying: 'OK, let's go back on Saturday.'

But what actually happens is that they get back home and immediately start looking on the internet again. Inevitably, they will see something else that takes their fancy and your chance of making a sale has all but evaporated.

Call them that same evening

That's why I would urge you to consider following up all those customers who leave without buying on the very same evening. Salespeople are often reluctant to do this, for fear of bugging the customer. And in all fairness, if all you are doing is getting on the phone to say, 'What do you think?' or, 'What are your thoughts?' then you probably are.

There is a simple rule in life: if we want something, we have to give before we receive. If you want love, you need to give it. If you want respect, you need to give it. And if you want information, you need to give it.

Structuring The Call

So, the follow up phone call needs to go something like this:

> 'Hello Mr or Mrs Customer, this is Simon calling from Toyota...'

In this call we're just going to say Toyota not Symco Toyota. Any ideas why? Sometimes the customer will ask which one and they've just told you they've been shopping around.

> '... sorry for disturbing you so soon...'

Always apologise first,

> '... but my reason for calling is, I forgot to tell you the car you're looking at has the full-size spare wheel, not just the foam inflation kit. Did I tell you that?'

It doesn't matter if they say, 'yes you did,' or, 'no you didn't,' it's just your excuse to call. By saying, 'I forgot to tell you' it means the call is more likely to be perceived as being for their benefit rather than yours.

> '... I'm sorry Mr Customer, I couldn't remember if I'd told you. I just didn't want you deciding without having all the facts.'

When you've got their attention, you then can go into:

> 'Experience has taught me that whenever you see something in a dealership that you like, it's only when you leave that you start thinking of any questions about it. Has it got this and has it got that, and so on. Can I ask you, Mr Customer, what other questions do you have about the car?'

Whatever you do, don't say: 'Do you have any other questions?' You're only ever going to get a yes or no answer (and probably no).

Get Them Thinking About Your Product

The true purpose of the question here is to get them thinking about your product or service again. For example, if I ask you, 'Did you enjoy your last holiday?' you can only say yes or no. But if I ask you, 'What was the best part of your last holiday?' now you've got to think about it. And that's exactly what I want my customers to do.

Then you can answer any questions that your customer actually has. Sometimes, of course, they will say they haven't really got any, and that's fine. It's your cue to move on, by saying: 'OK, great, well I have a question for you, if I may. Shall we secure that for you?' Or 'Shall we go ahead with it?'

Or alternatively:

'Is that the car you would like to be driving for the next two or three years?'

Or for other industries:

'Is that the mobile home that you'd really like to be going on holiday with?'

'Is that the kitchen you would really like to see in your house?'

Notice how I am trying to get them to take mental ownership here.

If you think that might be too strong for a particular customer you're dealing with, try this instead: 'OK great, well I've got a question for you. On a scale of one to ten, how do you rate that car overall? About an eight? OK, great, what would it have to do differently to make that a ten?'

Or: 'On a scale of one to ten – ten being that's the car you'd like to be driving, and one being it's not the right one for you – how would you rate it?'

Followed by: 'OK, great, what would have to change to make it a perfect ten?'

This is a great way of uncovering the customer's true objection – which made them want to go away and think about it in the first place.

There can be real power in putting a distance between you and the customer by speaking to them on the phone. Some people, face-to-face, can be reluctant to tell you what their real objection is. But over the phone, for some reason, it often comes out more easily.

Overcoming The Voicemail Problem

However, most of the follow up calls that salespeople make tend to sound something like this:

'Hi Mr Customer, you were in over the weekend, you were looking at that caravan. I just wanted to ask you if you had any more questions about it? No? OK, well if you do, here's my phone number, please don't hesitate to give me a call. Thank you very much, goodbye.'

They're not going to call you back and you're not going to see them again. It's also difficult to call them back again with the same sort of spiel, and if you do, you'll get nowhere. They'll probably start diverting your calls to voicemail as well. The chances of a customer responding to a message like this is virtually zero – because you've given them no real reason to call you back.

Running into voicemail is a perennial problem that salespeople face. What can you do about it? Most people who can afford to buy big-ticket items tend to work! And so they might be out during the day. They might get home late, for example. The first thing to try is calling at different times of the day.

Arouse Their Curiosity

Essentially, there are two types of voicemail message you can leave. The first one is designed to arouse their curiosity: 'Hi Mr Customer, it's Simon from Symco. Would you please give me a call regarding that Audi you were looking at? I've got some really good news for you.'

That's all you need to say. Put a bit of curiosity in the customer's mind.

> 'Hi Mr Customer, it's Simon from Symco. My phone number is 07123 456 789. That's 07123 456 789 [always repeat your number when leaving a voicemail message]. Would you give me a call please about the car we were looking at, I've got some really good news for you.'

The key to this one is the 'good news' element. Of course, you need to make sure that, if they do call you back, you have some good news for them – something about your product or service that you didn't tell the customer before.

Hang Up Halfway Through!

If that doesn't work for you, here's an alternative. It's one that helped me to land my biggest ever sales training contract, with a major car manufacturer. You can imagine how many training companies are trying to get their foot in the door with large companies. And the person I needed to speak to was using voicemail to screen his calls. If I simply left a message with my name, number and reason for the call, there wouldn't be much chance of him calling me back. He must get several of these calls every week. So instead, I found out the name of his boss from one of his manufacturer's franchised dealers, who I had worked quite closely with, and left the following message:

> 'Hi Geoff, my name's Simon Bowkett. I run a sales training company called Symco Training. My phone number's 07123 456 789. That's 07123 456 789. I'm calling because I was speaking to Paul Brayley and he suggested that yourself or Phil would be the right person to...'

And on the 'to' I hung up. He's heard half the message – and his boss's name. Will he call back now? Straight away he did. In fact, he was so quick that he caught me a little off guard.

And when he called, I assumed he'd heard the whole message.

> 'Thanks for calling me back Geoff, when's a good time for us to get together? Is it going to be this week or later on next week now?'
>
> 'It'll have to be later next week now, but what was it actually regarding?'
>
> 'Oh, sorry about that. It's just that we've completed a very successful sales training course for Paul Brayley. I wanted to stop by and tell you about the results we've had and what we could do for the whole network. Now you did say next week, is that going to be more Thursday or Friday?'

How rude would he have to be now, not to take the call and schedule an appointment?

You can only use this one once, of course. And use it when all else has failed because some people still don't always call back. I would use the curiosity approach first, and leave this one up my sleeve.

NINE

Are We There Yet?

Fifteen years ago, I was bored waiting for Emma to do some shopping, wearing a tatty old pair of jeans, an old pair of boots and a North Queensland Cowboys Rugby League jersey – I wasn't going to buy suit, but a salesperson approached me while I was flicking through some racks of suits. He asked me a question I couldn't not answer: 'Do you normally wear a double-breasted or single-breasted suit?' An alternative question!

I was just about to say, 'I was just looking,' but before I got the words out, he said, 'Just to let you know all the suits on that rack are double-breasted or blazers. All our single-breasted suits are on this rack here. The suits on the back wall are our core line product, we make the fabric ourselves, so if you ever have to get a new pair of trousers, we'll always have the fabric. That rack at the front is the sales rack, you might want have a look because there are some really good offers, up to

50% off. So, make yourself at home and have a look around.'
Signposting.

I left the double-breasted suits and went to look at the single-breasted suits. The salesman left me alone for about one minute while he tidied up some ties, keeping an eye on me, then he caught me with another alternatives question: 'Do you normally wear a lighter or a darker suit? The only reason I ask is that we've got some great lighter suits on the sales rack – lighter in weight and colour. We're trying to get rid of some summer stock.'

I went over and had a look at the sales rack, but there was nothing I liked, so I went back to the darker, single-breasted suits. I qualified myself.

He then hit me with a genius alternative question: 'If you *were* replacing a suit would you be replacing a work suit or a casual suit?' Now because I have absolutely no idea what a casual suit is, I replied with, 'A work suit.' And he followed up with, 'Oh, what work do you do?'

'I'm a sales trainer.'

He stepped back, 'You're not one of those mystery shoppers, are you? They've started coming in with hidden cameras and everything.'

'No, don't worry, I work in the motor trade.'

'I've always wanted to work in the motor trade.'

I don't know if he did or he didn't, but he was building rapport, qualifying the customer and not the deal.

He continued to qualify me, 'Oh, I'm sorry, I didn't introduce myself, I'm Simon.'

'I'm Simon as well.'

'Well, I'll always remember that. I've never seen you here before, where do you normally buy your suits?'

Now the ego of the puppy dog started to talk: 'Well, I normally buy Hugo Boss suits...'

Let me tell you the truth, I have never owned a Hugo Boss suit in my life. I bought my last suit from Bicester Outlet Village, it was shite and I wore the arse out of it. The salesman got the ego of my puppy dog talking and was working out my budget, continuing to qualify the customer and not the deal.

'Simon, do you travel a lot for your work?' I confirmed I did. 'Mainly by road or by air?' Emma and I had just started the company and all my travel was by road. The suit salesman then asked, 'How many miles a year are you doing?' I was doing about 40,000 miles a year, racing from gigs in Edinburgh one day to Plymouth the next.

I know he's used this next phrase with hundreds of people before and hundreds after: 'I'm willing to bet you've got a whole wardrobe of suits with the jackets perfectly good but you've worn the trousers out. Simon, what you need is something like this...' and he turned and walked.

What did I have to do? Follow him.

'Because you travel so much you need something like this, a bird's eye weave, which has more texture in it. While you're driving you're perspiring and that moisture gets into the garment, especially if you have leather seats. That moisture compresses the fibres and that's why you get that sheen. Also, you see this suit?' and he pulled at the material, making his knuckles go white, 'You see when I release the material the crease just falls out? That's because it's a quality wool suit and they last so much longer. We also recommend you get two pairs of trousers which more than doubles the length of ownership of your suit.' Simon the suit salesman continued to present the features, advantages, and benefits of their suits to build value and comparison.

He had his attitude just right, talking to a scruffy guy wearing an old pair of jeans. He'd already done a great meet and greet, he'd qualified me, he thinks he knows my current situation (Hugo Boss), he's done the presentation and now he's into the demonstration.

'Are you a 40 Regular, something like that?' and he put a jacket on me to try. He then gets a 40 Regular, dark, single-breasted suit and hangs it in the changing room. He carefully unwrapped a 15½ inch shirt, I protested, and he said, 'Simon you can't try the suit on with that jersey, it just wouldn't be right.' Then he looked down at my scruffy boots, 'What size are you?' He got on the phone and called the girl in the shoe shop downstairs; 'Bring me up a pair of black Oxford brogues, size 9.' I protested that I could try the suit with my socks, 'No, Simon it just wouldn't look right. It's no problem at all.' He's increasing the value, building in some bolt-ons and extras.

I went into the changing room and there's a suit, a shirt, a pair of brogues and two ties.

I tried it all on except for the tie. I looked at the sleeve to see the price and gulped. Then I reminded myself that whatever I spent on a suit, Emma was probably spending the same on shoes, or *a* shoe!

I went out of the cubicle and before I could say anything Simon the suit salesman said: 'No, that's not right. It's a German cut which I selected when you said you liked Hugo Boss suits, it's very straight up and down. You need something more tailored.' And he went and got another suit!

Two suits! I went to Chester not to buy a suit! And now I'm trying on a second suit, I even put the tie on. I liked it, I felt good. I looked at the sleeve to see the price, and he'd taken it off. I had no idea what the suit cost, and now I had to go out there to find out the price.

Now, I'm a happily married man, but when I walked out of the changing room the girl from the shoe store was still there and she was a stunner. I'm not naïve, I know this pair has run the double act before, and after he patted me down, preened and tweaked the suit, he said the immortal words any guy wants to hear: 'Simon, if you don't pull in this... there's something wrong.' The shoe sales girl agreed. This guy was good, stroking the puppy dog's ego and building huge mental ownership.

Then came the master alternatives close: 'Simon, do you want to take the suit, with the shirt and the shoes? Or do you want to take the suit by itself?' I didn't even know the price. I felt nauseous when he told me, 'You see Simon, that includes the extra pair of trousers we talked about. But, why don't you just get the suit and come back for the extra pair of trousers when you need them. That makes sense, doesn't it?'

He's got me, because if I say that makes sense, I've just bought a suit. If I say that doesn't make sense, I've just bought a suit and two pairs of trousers!

I've told that story hundreds of times and people always think that I'd never buy from that suit salesman again, but since 2000

I've *only* bought from Simon. If he'd lied about the quality of the suit I would never go back.

But more importantly, if he didn't have a process, I would never have bought the first suit.

Conclusion

In the first half of the book we talked about the four fundamentals of comparison, value, scarcity, and urgency, and how the right combination at the right time can help you make a sale and ensure the customer is satisfied. We covered getting your mindset right, understanding your customer's mindset, and how to build rapport with great questions.

In the second part of the book I shared my process that will help you stay motivated and keep you working towards your goal. We travelled through the four waypoints on the Road to a Sale and I gave you some of my personal word tracks. These word tracks are powerful: make them your own, use them, test them, and come up with some new variations.

Remember, this is a journey – you'll always be learning as you go along. I find selling can be the lowest paid easy work or the highest paid hard work. Be a student of sales. Study people and work out what makes people tick. Some of the best salespeople I know are people watchers.

Remember, you're not in the motorcar business – you're in the people business.

Now I've got even more great things for you. Over on our website there are plenty of tools and downloads available for you, including the printable cheat sheets of the Sales Word Tracks and when to use them. I've also prepared a special bonus chapter: *7 Words to Avoid & What to Say Instead*. Here's the link www.symcotraining.co.uk/bookresources.

Acknowledgements

Thanks to all my clients, you know how much you help me with your enthusiasm and support, you're all part of this story.

From my first boss, Mel Death (yes, I did start working for Mr DEATH in the motor industry) and Tony Ireland, who got me started on this crazy journey and helped mould me; to David Martin at the Markee Group, who I am proud to call a friend and mentor; there are too many partners, colleagues and collaborators to mention you all, but I want you to know I appreciate you.

None of this would have been possible without the support of my wife, Emma, and my family, as I race around the world delivering and developing training and keynote speeches. Thank you!

The Author

Simon Bowkett began his professional career in motor vehicle sales in Australia. Simon moved to the UK in 1995 to broaden his experience and was rapidly promoted into management and senior management, culminating in training and consultancy. He quickly established a reputation as a top trainer and motivator, attracting client after client by word of mouth. Many are still with him today, and these are among some of the best performing dealership sites and groups in the UK.

In 2000, he saw a gap in the market for trainers that could bring 'the real world' into training. Simon formed Symco Training to build a team of trainers and consultants who could bring practical experience and proven success to their training methods, all inheriting and delivering his ethos that 'There is no place for customer-shy trainers'.

Simon remains focused on the business, ensuring his material is kept current and relevant to today's challenges – resulting in a tried and tested approach and not the unproven world of theory. This guarantees the effectiveness of the material delivered in 'the real world' in your dealership, on the phone, or via email. Simon balances this with undertaking specific projects for manufacturers and dealer groups such as model launch training, special events and Train the Trainer sessions across Europe.

During his early career Simon was often referred to as Skippy or Skip, and the names have stayed with him ever since. His easy approach to getting the job done has resulted in long standing relationships – and it's not uncommon to hear many senior industry figures still refer to him as Skippy today.

Whether through his continual involvement in the ever-changing dealership environment or the vast quantity of online modules where his unique style is optimised, Simon, Skip, or Skippy has become an instantly recognisable face for Automotive Industry's Chairmen, Directors, General Managers, Sales/Aftersales Managers, Sales Executives and Service Advisors the length and breadth of the UK.

Simon has earned an exceptional reputation as a top speaker and presenter and is regularly asked to speak at motor industry events around the world. He has been a guest speaker at AM Sales and Aftersales Conferences, and has been providing monthly editorial features for an AM column since 2010, with engaging insights into highly topical and relevant stages of the sales and aftersales processes.

Simon's online content is accessed across Europe, America, Australia and New Zealand. The highly effective Sales Fitness Online Programmes have now exceeded over 100,000 delivered modules.

How Simon can help you

To get access to our online training programs, and a free trial, head over to www.symcotraining.co.uk/bookresources.

You'll also find our extra book resources there too, including the Excel spreadsheet to help you work out your figures and a free bonus chapter covering the words you shouldn't use: **7 Words to Avoid and What to Say Instead.**

For all our automotive training events, courses and consultancy: www.symcotraining.co.uk

If you want to book Simon as the keynote speaker for your next industry event or conference get in touch at book@simonbowkett.com

For more information: www.simonbowkett.com

Lightning Source UK Ltd.
Milton Keynes UK
UKHW021120270219
337822UK00004B/77/P